Mindsets and Practices of
the Contemporary School Counselor

Mindsets and Practices of the Contemporary School Counselor

A Practical Guide

Third Edition

Rita Schellenberg

ROWMAN & LITTLEFIELD
Lanham • Boulder • New York • London

Published by Rowman & Littlefield
An imprint of The Rowman & Littlefield Publishing Group, Inc.
4501 Forbes Boulevard, Suite 200, Lanham, Maryland 20706
www.rowman.com

6 Tinworth Street, London SE11 5AL

British Library Cataloguing in Publication Information Available

Library of Congress Cataloging-in-Publication Data Available

ISBN 978-1-4758-5134-2 (pbk : alk. paper)
ISBN 978-1-4758-5135-9 (electronic)

∞ ™ The paper used in this publication meets the minimum requirements of American
National Standard for Information Sciences Permanence of Paper for Printed Library
Materials, ANSI/NISO Z39.48-1992.

Printed in the United States of America

To countless others who have sought to quench seemingly insatiable desires to improve school counselor education and practice.

Contents

Preface

Evolutionary or Revolutionary?

If slow but steady wins the race, then our profession of school counselors and school counselors-in-training is in the lead! A bit more than a century young—yes, I said "young"—in profession time, we have made great strides toward unification and maturity. Remember, this is not a sprint but a marathon. It took the Egyptian civilization multiple centuries after unification to reach maturity—now that's quite a run!

The American School Counselor Association's national model reminds us of our extraordinary metamorphosis from "a position, to a service, to a program" (ASCA, 2012, p. vii). Still, the times they are a-changin'—to borrow a few of the fitting and golden words of Bob Dylan. Thanks to the continued and unbridled efforts of countless leaders, our next century promises to be just as evolutionary—perhaps revolutionary!

What we can broadly expect in this contemporary age of school counseling is a dedication to improvement. Addressing access, attainment, and achievement gaps will continue to be a significant challenge. Contemporary school counselors will continue to underscore the importance of responding to interventions, implementing empirically validated approaches, evaluating programs, and identifying research strategies for accountability and leadership.

Contemporary school counselors are called on to magnify the focus on comprehensive program structure, purpose, and management that is preventative and developmental in nature, promotes student achievement, and is both data driven and results oriented. There is a renewed emphasis on college and career readiness with the ASCA's mindsets and behaviors for student success (2014). For these reasons, school counselors are being asked to emphasize leadership, collaboration, advocacy, and systemic change, as illustrated in the ASCA national model's trademark diamond graphic (ASCA, 2012).

The concept of universal academic achievement has been redefined. We must therefore pay attention to strategies that not only identify and intervene in the lives of low-performing students, students with disabilities, and advanced-functioning students but also students who are not applying themselves in order to realize their full potential. These students are referred to as "invisible": introverted, shy, quietly distressed, or unmotivated (Cahill et al., 2018; Dong, Hwang, Shadieve, & Chen, 2017; Flett & Hewitt, 2013; Kerby & Wroughton, 2017; Matteson, 2014; Rosheim, 2018; Sink & Devlin, 2011). Continuing to uncover and nurture strengths that might otherwise lie dormant in these students will transform a population of students who are currently falling through the cracks—and every student is vital to fueling our nation and growing our next generation of world leaders.

Addressing the topic of spirituality and religion, historically viewed as taboo in schools, continues to gain momentum (Bohecker, Schellenberg, & Silvey, 2017; Farmer, 2017; Kimbel & Schellenberg, 2014; Magaldi-Dopman & Park-Taylor, 2014). School counselors and school counselors-in-training are being readied as crucial cultural agents to address the diverse spiritual needs of students and the developmental aspect of the human experience. Primary school counseling approaches for students of all developmental levels include supporting positive behaviors, exploring systems, and applying behavioral strategies to mediate academic and behavioral concerns. Strength-based counseling has become a commonly applied practice, exploring developmental assets in order to build resilience and fortify protection for students.

Technological advances continue to heighten the need for school counselors staying abreast of the websites and devices used daily by children and adolescents (Steele, Jacokes, & Stone, 2015). Understanding technology and what's hot in the digital world and social media, particularly for the school-age population you serve, is necessary to meeting the diverse needs of students. The explosion of gadgets and apps means that it is crucial for school counselors to promote their safe use. If we are to meet the needs of contemporary students, who literally have the world at their fingertips, then we must hold the mindset that our students can teach us how to help them!

This book promotes the transformation of our profession in what promises to be another unprecedented epoch by addressing established and developing best practices significant to maturing the school counseling profession. In this way, *Mindsets and Practices of the Contemporary School Counselor* is like its predecessors, *The New Era of School Counseling: A Practical Guide* (2013) and *The New School Counselor: Strategies for Universal Academic Achievement* (2008).

Also like its predecessors, this book uses a how-to approach with real-world applications that equip school counselors with the knowledge and strategies grounded in the ASCA national model (2012) and deemed essential by the Council for Accreditation of Counseling and Related Educational Programs (CACREP, 2016). The downloads that accompany this book (https://textbooks.rowman.com/schellenberg) provide school counselors with updated, user-friendly action plans and results report templates that reflect the newly created ASCA list of mindsets and behaviors (ASCA, 2014), as well as additional forms to meet the rigorous demands and highest standards of practice. A list of acronyms and glossary of frequently used terminology used in school settings are new to this edition.

The ability of this book to bridge contemporary theory and practice will also provide counselor educators and supervisors with experiential learning tools for optimal school counselor preparation. School administrators, too, will continue to find this brief resource helpful to understanding contemporary school counseling practices and counselors' current mindsets, roles, and functions.

So let us now embark on a new chapter in our profession, which promises continued positive outcomes. In doing so, we must keep in mind that the only thing constant is change; therefore, we cannot continue business as usual. We are still being called on to plow forward with unparalleled passion and selfless delight for creating a dynamic profession that frames school counselors as powerful and positive change agents. We might also stir this passion in others! Please feel free to play Survivor's 1982 worldwide, platinum, top-of-the-chart hit "Eye of the Tiger" if you like!

Acronyms and Abbreviations

Adapted from *The School Counselor's Study Guide for Credentialing Exams* (Schellenberg, 2018).

AACD	American Association for Counseling and Development
AACE	Association for Assessment in Counseling and Education
ACA	American Counseling Association
ACES	Association for Counselor Education and Supervision
ACSCI	Association of Computer-Based Systems for Career Information
ACT	American College Testing
ADHD	Attention-Deficit/Hyperactivity Disorder
AMCD	Association for Multicultural Counseling and Development
AOD	Alcohol and Other Drugs
APGA	American Personnel and Guidance Association
ASCA	American School Counselor Association
ASGW	Association for Specialists in Group Work
ASVAB	Armed Services Vocational Aptitude Battery
BIP	Behavior Intervention Plan
CACGS	Computer-Assisted Career Guidance Systems

CACREP	Council for Accreditation of Counseling and Related Educational Programs
CAPTA	Child Abuse Prevention and Treatment Act
CIDS	Career Information Delivery Systems
CPCE	Counselor Preparation Comprehensive Examination
CPS	Child Protective Services
CSCORE	Center for School Counseling Outcome Research and Evaluation
ELL	English Language Learners
ESEA	Elementary and Secondary Education Act
ESL	English as a Second Language
FERPA	Family Educational Rights and Privacy Act
GATB	General Aptitude Test Battery
GED	General Equivalency Diploma
HIPAA	Health Insurance Portability and Accountability Act
IDEA	Individuals with Disabilities Education Act
IEP	Individualized Education Program/Plan
KOIS	Kuder Occupational Interest Survey
LEP	Limited English Proficient
MBTI	Myers-Briggs Type Indicator
MOS	Microsoft Office Specialist
NBCC	National Board for Certified Counselors
NBPTS	National Board for Professional Teaching Standards
NCATE	National Council for Accreditation of Teacher Education
NCC	National Certified Counselor
NCDA	National Career Development Association
NCE	National Counseling Examination
NCLB	No Child Left Behind
NCSC	National Certified School Counselor
NCSCE	National Certified School Counselor Examination

NCTSC	National Center for Transforming School Counseling
NOCTI	National Occupational Competency Testing Institute
NRF	National Retail Federation
NSCTI	National School Counselor Training Initiative
NTE	National Teachers Examination
O*Net	Occupational Information Network
PIAT	Peabody Individual Achievement Test
PSAT	Preliminary Scholastic Aptitude Test
PSC	Professional School Counselor
PTA	Parent Teacher Association
PTSA	Parent Teacher Student Association
REBT	Rational Emotive Behavior Therapy
SAT	Scholastic Aptitude Test
SCA	Student Council Association
SCALE	School Counseling Analysis, Leadership and Evaluation
SCOPE	School Counseling Operational Plan for Effectiveness
SCORE	School Counseling Operational Report of Effectiveness
SDS	Self-Directed Search
SES	Socioeconomic Status
SII	Strong Interest Inventory
SOL	Standards of Learning
TSCI	Transforming School Counseling Initiative
WAIS	Wechsler Adult Intelligence Scale
WISC	Wechsler Intelligence Scale for Children

Chapter One

Contemporary Practices

A Preview

School counseling has historically been shaped by ever-changing social justice movements and educational reform initiatives, and over time, we have become more cautious in accommodating the latest trend in education reform. This new, third edition of the American School Counselor Association (ASCA) National Model (2012) continues to be the unifying professional framework that guides our ability to accommodate an array of reform agendas by maintaining our focus on growing a comprehensive school counseling program that takes a holistic and balanced approach to student development.

Traditionally, school counselors have viewed their primary function as the attempt to increase the academic achievement of students by removing physical, personal, social, emotional, and behavioral obstacles to learning using primarily "individual-focused interventions on behalf of selected students" (Eschenauer & Hayes, 2005). Conversely, school administrators have believed that school counselors should function more systemically and "work with students to build skills that have a direct impact on school related work and functioning" (Shoffner & Williamson, 2000, p. 128). This fundamental philosophical difference, coupled with the failure of school counselors to appropriately articulate their roles and functions, resulted in a lack of understanding of what school counselors do and, more importantly, how they are making a positive difference in the lives of students, families, and the communities we serve.

The powerful impetus behind crucial, fundamental change in the school counseling profession was prompted by a 1987 report published by the American Counseling Association (ACA) entitled "School Counseling: A Profession at Risk." The undeniable and disturbing realities outlined by the ACA regarding a profession viewed as unnecessary prompted immediate and unremitting action on the part of concerned stakeholders. Thanks to this report, things are changing, but we are not out of the woods yet. The profession has closed the philosophical divide and more closely aligned school counseling with the overall mission of schools, but some in their ranks are resistant to change.

In most states across the country, counselors are no longer viewed as a nice but unnecessary part of school curriculum. They have joined with school teachers, administrators, and other K–12 school specialists as part of a united front to change the nature of their profession. Traditionalists are called to jump on board the new, shared vision that is guiding contemporary school counselors into the next era as they help establish comprehensive school counseling programs that promote academic achievement while also balancing the holistic needs of students.

Terminology helps to define a profession and strengthen professional identity. Terms such as "guidance services" and "guidance counselor" are now considered old-fashioned and no longer reflect the comprehensive nature of modern school counseling programs and their dual roles of both educator and counselor. It is concerning, however, that even after so many years of evolution in the nature of their roles that many within and outside of the school community continue to use these outdated terms that reflect the stale profession of a bygone era instead of the dynamic profession it has become.

Contemporary school counselors are called on to change the language of the profession, promoting the new title of school counselor rather than guidance counselor and their professional services as school counseling services instead of guidance services (discussed in chapter 3) to reflect the changed roles and more comprehensive functions. This change also calls for building alliances with school administrators, who understand how the profession has evolved and therefore appreciate how the change in school counselors' titles and language aids in sustaining the profession (Duarte & Hatch, 2015).

School counselors can begin this building process by providing administrators with a thorough understanding of contemporary school counseling in accordance with the ASCA National Model and the Council for Accreditation of Counseling and Related Educational Programs (CACREP). It is crucial to reveal the evidence of outcomes that demonstrate how today's school counseling programs are contributing to academic and postsecondary achievement as well as holistic student development and well-being—reflecting our dual contemporary roles and functions. Only then can they continue to influence the deep-seated beliefs of administrators, teachers, and other educational specialists who may still view school counseling programs as ancillary. The trajectory of the school counseling profession has been altered. Now, it must continue to work to sustain comprehensive, developmentally appropriate, and culturally sensitive school counseling programs that focus on both student development and academic achievement. Ralph Waldo Emerson may have said it best: "This time, like all other times, is a very good one, if we but know what to do with it."

FORCES SHAPING A MATURING PROFESSION

Now is not the time for complacency. The past offers insights from which we can learn, the inspiration from which we can grow, the strength to go forward, and the knowledge to pass along to future generations. Change can be frightening, but the courage to change can result in great things. There are several areas to focus on as school counselors move to transform their profession.

Transforming School Counseling Initiative and the ACA

Soon after the publication of "School Counseling: A Profession at Risk" (ACA, 1987), ASCA began publishing monographs, position papers, role statements, revised program philosophies, and a series of recommendations to help position school counselors as key players in educational reform initiatives. ASCA adopted national standards for school counselors and developed a national model to aid in unifying the profession and serving as a guide to comprehensive developmental practices. The Education Trust (1997) as well introduced the Transforming School Counseling Initiative (TSCI), a new paradigm that began emphasizing the importance of school counseling leadership, support for academic- and systems-focused programming, and the need to make adequate yearly progress. Together, ASCA and the TSCI served as visionaries by redefining the roles and functions of school counselors that more closely align them with the academic mission of schools by shifting the focus of school counseling away from mental health and toward academic achievement, away from the individual student and toward the whole school.

Those attached to the traditional mental health–focused paradigm argue that this new model is too focused on academics, ignoring the mental health needs of students. Proponents of the new vision of school counseling argue, however, that the new paradigm does not represent an end to mental health services but rather focuses them to more fully meet the mental health needs of students by linking data-driven interventions to the overall mission and purposes of schooling while holding themselves accountable for their contributions to student outcomes (Brigman, Villares & Webb, 2017; Duarte & Hatch, 2015; Goodman-Scott, Betters-Bubon, & Donohue, 2016; Michel, Lorelle, & Atkins, 2017; Paisley & Hayes, 2003).

New vision school counseling requires a belief in the capacity of all students at varying developmental stages to reach their academic potential and overcome life's obstacles, enhancing their ability to enjoy meaningful futures in a global economy and technologically advanced world. This new generation of school counselor leaders engage in collaboration and consultation toward this end, taking a team approach to serving students and families by removing inequities and other barriers to academic achievement (Cholewa, Goodman-Scott, Thomas, & Cook, 2016; Havlik, Rowley, Puckett, Wilson, & Neasen, 2017; Mayes, Dollarhide, & Young, 2018; Moran & Bodenhorn, 2015). School counselors document their schools' practices and programming outcomes, including closing the achievement gap strategies, using action plans, lesson plans, and results reports (ASCA, 2012).

Prior to the TSCI, school counselor training programs generally applied a clinical, mental health pedagogy and an individual focus, with little or no emphasis on standards, systems, technology, the use of data, academic achievement, program evaluation, evidence-based practices, and data reporting. Therefore, many currently practicing school counselors lack the preparation and understanding of the roles and functions of the contemporary, academic-focused school counselor and the tools and approaches they need to succeed. Since practice informs academic theory, paradoxically, deficits in practice create deficits in school counselor education, resulting in the absence of applied new vision approaches and models for the optimal preparation of future school counselors.

While the TSCI was established with the express purpose of restructuring school counselor education at the graduate level, it recognizes the need to close this preparation gap between school counselors trained under the traditional model and those trained under the new model. For that reason, the TSCI partnered with Metropolitan Life Insurance Company (MetLife) to fund the development of the National School Counselor Training Initiative (NSCTI) and the National Center for Transforming School Counseling (NCTSC) located at www.edtrust.org/dc/tsc.

The NSCTI and NCTSC developed and disseminated four modules that instruct practicing school counselors in the components of the TSCI. These modules challenge traditional school counselor belief systems and demonstrate how school counselors can contribute to the high academic achievement of and obtain educational equity for all students through collaborative leadership and advocacy.

Center for School Counseling Outcome Research and Evaluation (CSCORE)

The Center for School Counseling Outcome Research and Evaluation (CSCORE, 2000), formerly known as the Center for School Counseling Outcome Research (CSCOR), was established during a TSCI summer conference for the purpose of providing school counselor leadership in establishing accountable practices. The center is part of the School of Education at the University of Massachusetts (www.umass.edu/school counseling).

The center focuses on providing resources to assist school counselors in grounding practices in research and standards, conducting program evaluation, and administering valid outcome measures. It publishes quarterly research briefs for school counseling practitioners to increase knowledge regarding ways in which school counselors can implement academic- and systems-focused practices and support strategies for closing achievement gaps. CSCORE specifically advocates for contemporary school counseling practices by (1) assisting efforts to ensure that all students achieve academically, (2) emphasizing the importance of systemic interventions, and (3) focusing on the importance of using research to guide practice, monitor effectiveness, and evaluate student learning outcomes.

Association for Counselor Education and Supervision (ACES) and the Council for Accreditation of Counseling and Related Educational Programs (CACREP)

The Association for Counselor Education and Supervision (ACES) is a division of the ACA. Its purpose (www.acesonline.net) is to provide leadership and continuous improvement in the education, credentialing, and supervision of counselors in diverse specialty settings. Committed to the advancement of counselor education and supervision, ACES began the accreditation of counseling programs, which laid the foundation for its successor, the Council for Accreditation of Counseling and Related Educational Programs (CACREP).

In 1978, CACREP (www.cacrep.org) was formed to standardize training, and it now functions as the primary accrediting body for counselor education programs. In 2001, it published standards that reflected the new vision's academic- and systems-focused paradigm. In 2009, CACREP revised those standards to continue reflecting the contemporary practices of counseling and counseling specialties, taking into account current developments and future trends. The 2009 standards emphasize the professional identity of the school counselor and the importance of measuring student learning outcomes. Revised again in 2016, CACREP continues its emphasis on professional identity and a unified counseling profession.

CACREP provides counselor education programs with uniform, minimal competencies for the optimal preparation of school counselors and requires demonstrated knowledge in eight core areas of counselor education: professional orientation and ethical practice, social and cultural diversity, human growth and development, career development, helping relationships, group work, assessment, and research and program evaluation. Those studying to become school counselors must also master thirty-four professional knowledge and skills standards in three dimensions: foundations, contextual, and practice (CACREP, 2016).

These school counseling specialty standards emphasize education and training in developing a comprehensive, developmentally appropriate school counseling program using evidence-based prevention and intervention practices that meet the diverse needs of students. The standards further underscore the importance of using a program model (e.g., ASCA National Model) in both school counselor education and school counseling practices. CACREP also spotlights the importance of academic outcomes and demonstrating the use of data-driven and data-producing programs as well as program evaluation in school counseling practices. The standards further emphasize the importance of identifying and removing personal and systemic barriers to academic achievement.

Now more than forty years old, CACREP continues to grow and provides unity and leadership to the discipline of counselor education for both residential and online programs (Ritchie & Bobby, 2011; Snow, Lamar, Hinkle, & Speciale, 2018). "CACREP has become a university magnet with schools across the country seeking its stamp of approval. Indeed, if school counselor education were a religion, CACREP would be our bible, with counselor educators striving to live by the word" (Schellenberg, 2018, p. 7).

National Board for Certified Counselors (NBCC)

Gladding (2001) defines certification as the process by which an agency, government, or association officially grants recognition to an individual for having met certain professional qualifications that have been developed by the profession. NBCC (www.nbcc.org) is the national professional certification board that monitors the certification system for counselors and maintains a national register of certified counselors. In addition to national credentialing, NBCC examinations are used by more than forty-eight states to credential professional counselors on the state level. NBCC was created by the ACA, and both organizations work closely to advance the profession of counseling and maintain high standards of excellence.

The NBCC administers specialty counseling credentials such as the National Certified School Counselor (NCSC) credential, first awarded in 1991. The National Certified Counselor (NCC) credential is a prerequisite or corequisite for the NCSC. School counselors who hold the NCSC credential have demonstrated competence in areas specific to contemporary school counseling and demonstrate a high level of professional commitment that goes beyond required state licensing. The NCSC is a product of a collaborative effort between key professional counseling organizations and supported by CACREP and ACES.

The NBCC and the National Board for Professional Teaching Standards (NBPTS) began working together to create an advanced credential for school counselors that would tie school counseling standards to the NBPTS requirements. Negotiations ended unsuccessfully in 2003, however, when NBCC would not agree to (1) an advanced counselor credential controlled by a sixty-three-member board of teachers with just one school counselor representative, (2) an advanced counselor credential that does not require a master's degree, and (3) an advanced school counseling credential that is not a collaborative effort that includes all professional associations, accreditation, and certification organizations in counseling.

The NBPTS is a teacher certification board and association that promotes the school counselor as educator, whereas CACREP, NBCC, and ASCA are counselor accrediting, certification, and professional associations that promote the school counselor's professional identity as counselor as most important. Although understanding that school counselors are counselors first and foremost, CACREP, NBCC, and ASCA recognize both roles, educator and counselor, in defining the profession. School counselors focus on academic achievement, but they do so in relation to the provision of sound counseling services. Educators understand the priorities—student safety first and always. Counselor educators, parents, teachers, and school administrators desire instructional competence in a school counselor, but they also need clinical counseling competence in a school counselor, who is often the only mental health professional in the school building. Unfortunately, even with the application of a collaborative model, the only counselor a troubled child or adolescent may ever see is the school counselor.

An advanced school counselor credential that is not governed primarily by the counseling profession may not inspire the public's confidence in the school counselor's clinical ability to meet the personal, social, and emotional needs of children. This is particularly significant in a charged climate where the public's confidence in our educational system is already wavering. Parents are not only questioning the ability of public schools to successfully educate their children but also the ability of public schools to identify and effectively intervene in situations in which troubled students may threaten the safety of their child.

Whether one believes that a school counselor is a counselor placed in a school setting or an educator who applies counseling skills, the counseling component and counselor identity must be equally advanced and empowered. As such, one credential must not be pitted against or supported more than the other. Both credentials are valuable in establishing the school counselor's advanced knowledge and expertise in counseling and teaching. Currently, however, most states provide incentives only for the NBPTS-certified school counselor, perpetuating the school counselor's blurred perceptions of professional identity. Exclusive support for the primarily teacher-controlled NBPTS school counseling credential may also be perceived as an implied belief that instructional competence supersedes clinical and counseling competence.

The US House of Representatives Committee on Appropriations voiced concern regarding the NBPTS's credentialing of school counselors, encouraging the NBPTS to retain its intended focus—to improve the skills and credentials of classroom teachers (U.S. House of Representatives, 2006). Acting on this concern, the House Committee on Appropriations has provided more flexibility to the Department of Education regarding the earmarking of advanced credential funding. This House Committee action may open the door to school administrators and all stakeholders to advocate for the recognition of the NBCC's school counselor credential, as well as NBPTS's credential, when providing incentives and financial supplements for the advanced credentialing of school counselors.

American School Counselor Association (ASCA)

ASCA provides professional development, leadership, advocacy, research, publications, and resources to school counselors worldwide. ASCA calls for an alignment with academic achievement missions and programming that includes strategies to help close the achievement gap. The ASCA National Model (2012) is supported by CACREP, professional school counseling associations, and a substantial body of research and literature. Embracing an academic-focused model for school counseling is further supported by research that links student academic success to collaborative school cultures that exude an academic emphasis (Goddard, Hoy, & Woolfolk, 2000). Many of their resources do not require association membership in order to gain access at www.schoolcounselor.org.

ASCA adopted national standards (Campbell & Dahir, 1997) and created a national model (ASCA, 2012) to include those standards. Recently, it replaced the 1997 standards with the ASCA Mindsets and Behaviors for Student Success (ASCA, 2014). The ASCA national model aids in unifying school counselors' professional identity and practices and serves as a framework from which to establish accountable, comprehensive, developmental school counseling programs. School counseling programs that demonstrate fidelity to the ASCA Model can apply to be a Recognized ASCA Model Program (RAMP). Programs that garner the RAMP stamp of approval have demonstrated an alignment with this nationally accepted professional model and thereby their school's commitment to leading a data-driven, comprehensive school counseling program. This national model provides standards, competencies, and indicators for facilitating student development and also includes school counselor performance standards that reflect contemporary roles and functions in school counseling practices.

ASCA provides school counseling practitioners and counselor educators with interactive tools such as the School Counseling Analysis, Leadership and Evaluation (SCALE) Research Center. School counselors can link to the center from the main ASCA Web page. SCALE provides resources to support results-based, comprehensive school counseling programs and identifies potential research partners, grants, and professional development opportunities. ASCA Scene also allows school counselors and counselor educators to interact with others and the system to get information and resources to support professional roles and functions, providing a massive file cabinet of materials for practice, discussion groups, webinar listings, and membership profiles for professional networking. Lastly, the ASCA U Specialist Trainings program offers certifications in many areas of specialty not limited to bullying, trauma and crisis, ethics, cultural competence, grief and loss, leadership, and anxiety. School counselors and other stakeholders are encouraged to visit www.schoolcounselor.org for a complete list of trainings and professional development opportunities.

ACHIEVING ACADEMIC-FOCUSED SCHOOL COUNSELING

Failure of the traditional mental health model to align school counseling with the mission of schools and to demonstrate an impact on academic achievement is chronicled in professional literature and exemplified in the historical exclusion of school counselors from educational reform agendas. The direction of the profession has been slow to turn, but it is turning.

It takes time to apply theory to practice. Attaching school counseling to school reform initiatives and to the educational system as a whole requires changes in counselor education, practice, and leadership, as well as practical tools and approaches. School counselors have been astutely careful not to neglect the personal, social, and emotional needs of children and adolescents while they also attend to academic achievement.

Time has not been the only barrier to more academic-focused practices. Some counselor educators and school counseling practitioners have been reluctant to support the paradigm switch, preferring to adhere to the traditional model for what is likely a multitude of reasons, including a lack of motivation toward change in general. For these die-hard traditionalists not hard-wired to change, the shift has been explosive. Providentially, a lack of support from school counseling professionals intent upon traditional practices has been met by an unequivocal force—school administrators.

School Administrator and School Counselor Leadership Alliance

The involvement and support of school administrators is essential to building a comprehensive school counseling program that is effective, evolving, and systems-focused. School counseling alliances have been forged, and they are working to switch the paradigm and reverse the direction of passé school counseling practices.

School boards, superintendents, and school principals determine the roles and functions of school counselors within each school. Therefore, implementation of a comprehensive school counseling program that balances the career, academic, and personal–social development of students depends upon the acceptance, support, and collective leadership of school administrators and school counseling practitioners.

Historically, school administrators have come from teacher backgrounds and received minimal training in educational leadership programs on the perspectives of school personnel other than teachers. As such, school administrators have had limited opportunities to fully understand the roles and functions of the school counselor as delineated by the school counseling profession.

School counselors, many of whom were schooled under the traditional pedagogy prior to the establishment of the ASCA national model, are also unable to clearly articulate the contemporary roles, functions, identity, goals, and direction of our profession. As a result, many school administrators have been relegated to the position of spectator, despite supervisory responsibilities and a vested interest in integrating this disconnected and specialized subset into the educational system.

Therefore, the first step toward establishing a school counselor and school administrator alliance is to arrive at a mutual understanding of the independent and interdependent functions of each of the system's components. Appreciating this interconnectedness and understanding that changes in one component (school counseling programs) have consequences for the entire school mission is vital to positive systemic change. Fittingly, the systems-integration philosophies of W. Edwards Deming have been likened to the contemporary leadership role of school administrators.

> Systems thinking is like conducting a piece of music for an orchestra. . . . Each element can function apart from the others. . . . The flute solo may be pleasant, the percussion powerful, the strings, in perfect harmony . . . it is the work of the conductor who pulls all the parts together into one beautiful song. Only then do the musicians—and the audience members—get the full and intended effect. When the parts are working together as a thriving whole under the direction of a skilled school leader, the district becomes more effective. (Sutton, 2006, p. 47)

School administrators are continuously challenged to ensure a rigorous, standards-based curriculum, heighten accountability, and integrate specialized resources and manpower to bring about monumental systemic change in education. School counselors are being called upon to engage those specialized skills in counseling and education and to align with the larger school mission and directly impact global student achievement using accountable practices. For the first time in history, school administrator and school counselor paradigms, perspectives, and goals are homogenous, making leadership alliances not only probable but uniquely powerful.

SUMMARY

In order to continue to grow as a profession and to meet the diverse needs of students in today's educational climate, school counselor education and practice must maintain the paradigm shift from the traditional mental health–focused model that serves a select few to the academic-focused paradigm that serves the many and better aligns with the academic-achievement mission of schools. Despite support for the academic-focused paradigm from the major forces that shape the profession of school counseling, some counselor educators and practitioners are content to continue promoting the outdated, unsuccessful individual-based mental health model. Proponents of the new model must place their emphasis on school administrator–school counselor alliances to ensure the implementation of comprehensive school counseling programs that focus on total student development while also enhancing academic achievement through both direct and indirect student services.

School counselors should promote needs-driven, standards-based, accountable programming that aligns comprehensive school counseling programs with overall academic achievement missions and contribute to closing the access, achievement, and attainment gaps.

Chapter Two

A Systems Focus

Once a profession focused on providing guidance services and responding to the individual mental health needs of a select few, the "guidance counselor" paradigm switch to a more balanced approach was a game changer for the school counseling profession. The passage to comprehensive school counseling services for all that align with the academic achievement mission of schools has been an extraordinary journey.

Collaboration and consultation with stakeholders—namely school administrators, parents, teachers, and members of the community—continue to take center stage in developing and strengthening school counseling programs that meet the customized, diverse, and holistic needs of students and unique school environments. School counseling programs don't belong to school counselors: they belong to the stakeholders. Accordingly, ASCA recommends establishing an advisory council in which stakeholder membership is representative of the community's diversity. The ASCA National Model (2012) provides guidelines for creating a viable school counseling advisory council that promotes system perspectives by involving diverse stakeholders. Identifying stakeholder needs also requires the ability to create and conduct needs assessments and identify and analyze existing relevant data sources within and outside of the school. Information obtained from data collection and analysis aids school counselors in designing or redesigning programs for targeted topics and populations and allows for continuous program improvement.

Chapter 2

DATA-DRIVEN PROGRAM PLANNING

The powerful smack of hard data provides us with the sobering clarity needed to make informed decisions that positively impact comprehensive, developmentally appropriate, and culturally sensitive school counseling programs. The study of data can reveal unmet stakeholder needs, inequities in programming and practices, and other barriers to academic achievement and student development (Kim, Fletcher, & Bryan, 2018; Young & Kaffenberger, 2016). ASCA (2012; 2016b) calls for school counselors to collect three types of data:

1. process data
2. perception data
3. outcome data when evaluating programs/services.

Process data identifies the manner in which the program was implemented and how many participants were impacted. It endeavors to answer the question "What did you do, and for whom?" and provides evidence that an event occurred (ASCA, 2012, p. 51). Perception data measures what participants think they know, believe, or can do as well as attitudes, knowledge, and skills attained by participants using self-report measures such as needs assessments and before (pretest) and after (post-test) intervention surveys. Perception data endeavors to answer the question "What do people think they know, believe, or can do?" (ASCA, 2012, p. 51).

While perception and process data are useful for program improvement and duplication, outcome data is essential to establishing how the school counseling activity made a difference and to what extent—in other words, its effectiveness. Outcome data demonstrates program impact and endeavors to answer the question "So what?" (ASCA, 2012, p. 52). Outcome data supports the need for a particular kind of counseling service, such as classroom guidance lessons and group counseling, and is used to demonstrate the impact of the counseling service with objective, standardized data. Examples of outcome data include attendance and graduation rates, promotion and retention rates, standardized test scores, and grade point averages.

School counselors have access to a robust cornucopia of existing data sources that offer many opportunities for needs identification, accountable program planning, implementation, and evaluation. When using existing data sources, school counselors look for patterns and inconsistencies. The following list includes potential achievement and behavioral data sources generally available to school counselors.

- academic portfolio goals completion
- attendance rates
- career and technical education program participation
- career assessments
- career portfolio—career action plan goal completion
- classroom performance data
- college acceptance rates
- conflict resolution/peer mediation records
- consultation
- course enrollment patterns
- demographic data
- discipline records
- dropout rates
- drug violations
- expulsion records
- financial data
- grade reports
- graduation rates
- homework completion records
- industry certification participation/pass rates
- interest inventories
- needs assessment
- nontraditional program track (GED, job corps, etc.)
- parent/community school involvement—volunteer data
- parent-teacher conference records
- pre- and post-program knowledge/skills measure
- program completions (GED, honors)
- promotion and retention rates
- PTA/PTSA attendance rates
- scholarship records
- school event attendance rates
- scores on the GED official practice test
- self-assessment
- standardized assessment data/test scores
- student community service/volunteer data

- student extracurricular activities participation
- suspensions (in-school)
- suspensions (out-of-school)
- time-out records

Data-based decision making in education has been defined as the "process of collecting, analyzing, reporting, and using data for school improvement" (Poynton & Carey, 2006, p. 121), and school counselors can leverage the power of information technology to inform and improve educational practices.

Many data-based decision-making models both within and outside of schools are available for school counselors to use as a framework for facilitating the process (Duarte & Hatch, 2015). It is prudent to capture data from multiple sources in order to clarify needs and identify levels of need for timely, successful programming. A combination of both existing data and needs assessment approaches can provide powerful support for programming.

Needs Assessment Instruments and Techniques

Stakeholder needs may be assessed using existing data, as previously noted, or by gathering data in the form of participant perceptions from the target population using a needs assessment instrument. Needs assessments techniques and instruments are time-honored means by which school counselors can identify and target relevant needs for appropriate programming. Needs assessments are generally used to systematically identify the needs of broader populations (e.g., students, teachers, parents, community agencies) and subpopulations (e.g., special education students, fifth-grade teachers, parents of gifted students, mental health agencies).

Needs assessments based on participant perceptions can take a formal tone or an informal tone. Assessment instruments and techniques may be written (e.g., surveys, questionnaires) or oral (e.g., interviews) and conducted in person, on the telephone, via the internet, or by mail. When assessing needs based on participant perception, the school counselor might elect to use focus groups, community forums, or key informants.

School counselors who use focus groups select multiple individuals who are representative of the population to be served—much like apple picking. In a structured or semi-structured format, diverse needs are collectively discussed, and the group prioritizes needs. If you have any bad apples, this is where you'll find out! Community forums have merit due to the inclusive nature of the approach. Any stakeholder wishing to be involved may participate. School counselors announce the topic to be discussed along with meeting dates and times. Those interested participate in much the same fashion as the focus group. The school counselor selects the key informants based on the potential participant's level of knowledge of the target population. The participant may or may not be a member of the population, but most have an in-depth knowledge of the target population. Key informants are typically surveyed individually or in small groups.

Initial needs assessments administered to adult stakeholders might begin with general questions, and the responses to those questions might suggest a need for more specific follow-up questions vital to targeting needs-driven programming and identifying best practices. The following sampling of questions would be considered appropriate for assessing the needs of upper elementary school students, adults, and students at the high school level:

- What school counseling services do you find helpful?
- What additional school counseling services would you find helpful?
- What are the strengths of the school counseling program?
- What suggestions do you have for possible improvements to the school counseling program?
- What questions do you have regarding the school counseling program and services?
- What are some ways you would like to become involved in the school counseling program?
- What barriers to student development have you observed or believe exist in our school?
- What suggestions do you have for the school counseling program for removing such barriers?

Needs assessments for children may be read aloud with interpretations depending upon developmental level. Needs assessments that make use of the check system are ideal for children and special-needs populations. For example, simply list the topics and have students place a check in the box beside the topic(s) of interest:

- Dealing with bullies
- Safety (including internet safety)
- Nutrition and health

- Study skills and organization
- Test-taking skills
- Making and keeping friends
- Self-control
- Managing time
- Managing anger
- Communication
- Career
- Conflict resolution/peer mediation (getting along)
- Problem solving
- Decision making (making good choices)
- Self-esteem (liking myself)
- Managing stress (expressing feelings)
- Setting and achieving goals
- Grief and loss
- Trauma and crisis
- Eating disorders
- College readiness

The check system is also easily administered. The school counselor may find it useful to combine elements of both structures based on intended purpose and population.

TRANSLATING NEEDS INTO GOALS
AND MEASURABLE OBJECTIVES

Once the school counselor understands systemic programming based on stakeholder needs, those needs are translated into goal(s) that are supported by measurable objectives. For example, a goal based on need might be to reduce school-wide conflict. This broad goal does not lend itself to measurement; that is the task of the objective. Therefore, once a goal(s) is established, specific and measurable objectives that support goal achievement are developed.

One possible objective supporting the goal of reducing school-wide conflict might be "students will be able to identify three conflict resolution strategies." The outcome might then be that at least three conflict resolution strategies must be included in the curriculum content. Research-supported curriculum development is discussed later in this chapter.

ASCA provides school counselors with broad goals (e.g., standards) and objectives (i.e., student competencies) that cover the three broad domains for a developmental comprehensive school counseling program. School counselors, however, must also develop their own more specific and measurable objectives based on stakeholder need. Understanding how to translate stakeholder needs into goals and measurable learning objectives is crucial to creating program content that targets those needs. The following is a method for creating measurable objectives using a (W)ho, (H)ow, and (W)hat process:

Who (**W**) are the participants receiving the program/intervention? *Who* examples:

- "Students will"
- "Teachers will"
- "Parents will"

How (**H**) will we know the behavior is achieved? *How* examples:

- "Students will identify"
- "Parents will be able to"
- "Teachers will develop"

What (**W**) is the desired behavior? *What* examples:

- "Students will identify five study skills strategies"
- "Parents will be able to define ADHD"
- "Teachers will develop five auditory teaching strategies"

RESEARCH-SUPPORTED CURRICULUM DEVELOPMENT

Once stakeholder needs are translated into goal(s) and measurable objectives, program content is created that supports those goal(s) and objectives. If the goal is to improve student study skills, for example, a measurable objective supporting this goal might be "students will identify five study skills strategies." The curriculum will include research-supported content and activities specific to achieving this objective. That is, the content will, in some manner, introduce five research-supported study skills strategies, ideally with this specific population in mind.

Let's consider the concept of self-esteem. Negative self-esteem has had a long and prosperous career in invading hearts and minds with self-destructive rubbish, making "self" our best friend or our worst enemy. The benefits of positive self-esteem are widely recognized (Bardhoshi, Duncan, & Erford, 2017; Schellenberg, 2018). With the help of research, school counselors reveal the link between self-esteem and personal, social, career, and academic development. The school counselor will seek to underscore the relationship between academic success and self-esteem to demonstrate a clear alignment with the academic mission of schools.

Once this link is established, research-supported interventions that have been successful in building a positive self-esteem are identified. Unlike the murmurs of idle gossip, research communicates factual information that demonstrates evidence-based techniques, models, and approaches, identifying what works and with whom—so-called best practices (Schellenberg, 2018). To apply best practices, school counselors critically evaluate important components of relevant studies such as (1) theoretical orientation, (2) target population, (3) intervention used, (4) method of data collection and analysis, and (5) results. Again, using the construct/topic of self-esteem as our example, the following questions might aid in guiding school counselors toward this end:

- Does a correlation exist between self-esteem and academic performance?
- What does the research say about the academic proficiency of students who have negative self-esteem versus those who have a positive self-esteem?
- Is poor self-esteem considered to be a barrier to academic achievement? If so, would it be logical to conclude that programs that enhance self-esteem remove a barrier to academic achievement?
- Which counseling and instructional interventions have been used in the past with positive outcomes?
- With what populations were the counseling and instructional interventions successful?

When developing curriculum, school counselors are sensitive to the diverse learning needs of students. School counselors accommodate the variety of learning styles and learning levels of students, and they are also careful to consider the theory of multiple intelligences when seeking to create lessons and group sessions geared toward holistic student development.

Howard Gardner (1983) contends that human cognition consists of eight independent yet interactive intelligences across a variety of disciplines. Gardner defines intelligence as "biopsychological potential to process information that can be activated in a cultural setting to solve problems or create products that are of value in a culture" (Gardner & Moran, 2006, p. 1). These eight intelligences (i.e., linguistic, logical-mathematical, musical, spatial, bodily kinesthetic, naturalistic, interpersonal, and intrapersonal) are described in table 2.1.

Table 2.1. Marzano's Nine Instructional Strategies.

Instructional Strategy	Characteristics
Identifying similarities and differences	Breaking concepts into similar and dissimilar pieces; representing concepts in graphic forms (e.g., Venn diagrams, charts, analogies)
Summarizing and notetaking	Conceptualizing presented material, then restating it in one's own words; when notetaking, more notes are better and allow time to process
Reinforcing effort and providing recognition	Show the connection between effort and achievement (e.g., share success stories, underscore student's achievements); recognize individual accomplishments and personalize them
Homework and practice	Amount of schoolwork should vary by grade level; homework schedule and setting should be consistent; homework provides practice; provide feedback on homework in a variety of ways
Nonlinguistic representations	Use with linguistic representations; nonlinguistic representations stimulate and increase brain activity; use tangible models and physical movement, and apply symbols to represent words and images
Cooperative learning	Has a positive impact on learning; vary group sizes and objectives
Setting objectives and providing feedback	Provide direction for learning; students should personalize goals and use contracts; feedback should be timely, specific, and rubric-based
Generating and testing hypotheses	Use general rules to make a prediction; students should explain their predictions

Cues, questions, and advanced organizers	Students use background knowledge to enhance learning; expose students to material prior to their learning (e.g., create a graphic image, tell a story)

Adapted from Marzano, R. J. (2004), *Building background knowledge for academic achievement: Research on what works in schools.* Alexandria, VA: Association for Supervision and Curriculum Development.

The interactive nature of multiple intelligences offers insight into the workings of the human mind. Whether intriguing or deeply disturbing, this information is nothing less than invaluable in developing and delivering curriculum that nurtures the diverse intelligences for optimal cognitive and affective learning experiences and sound career decision making.

Benjamin S. Bloom (1953) describes six classifications of learning levels progressing from the most basic to the most complex in hierarchical order: knowledge, comprehension, application, analysis, synthesis, and evaluation. Bloom's Taxonomy has been revised to associate specific verbs that represent ways to promote the development of higher-level thinking skills at each level (Anderson & Krathwohl, 2001) as illustrated in figure 2.1.

Robert Marzano's (2004) frequently applied instructional strategies have been empirically validated as approaches that build background knowledge and improve student achievement across grade levels. These strategies are listed in table 2.2.

Table 2.2. Marzano's Nine Instructional Strategies.

Instructional Strategy	Characteristics
Identifying similarities and differences	Breaking concepts into similar and dissimilar pieces; representing concepts in graphic forms (e.g., Venn diagrams, charts, analogies)
Summarizing and notetaking	Conceptualizing presented material, then restating it in one's own words; when notetaking, more notes are better and allow time to process
Reinforcing effort and providing recognition	Show the connection between effort and achievement (e.g., share success stories, underscore student's achievements); recognize individual accomplishments and personalize them
Homework and practice	Amount of schoolwork should vary by grade level; homework schedule and setting should be consistent; homework provides practice; provide feedback on homework in a variety of ways

Nonlinguistic representations	Use with linguistic representations; nonlinguistic representations stimulate and increase brain activity; use tangible models and physical movement, and apply symbols to represent words and images
Cooperative learning	Has a positive impact on learning; vary group sizes and objectives
Setting objectives and providing feedback	Provide direction for learning; students should personalize goals and use contracts; feedback should be timely, specific, and rubric-based
Generating and testing hypotheses	Use general rules to make a prediction; students should explain their predictions
Cues, questions, and advanced organizers	Students use background knowledge to enhance learning; expose students to material prior to their learning (e.g., create a graphic image, tell a story)

Adapted from Marzano, R. J. (2004), *Building background knowledge for academic achievement: Research on what works in schools.* Alexandria, VA: Association for Supervision and Curriculum Development.

Lastly, the theory of learning style contends that individuals have a propensity toward receiving and storing information using one or more of three sensory modalities: visual (e.g., pictures, written word), kinesthetic (e.g., body movement, tactile), and auditory (e.g., spoken word). It is important for school counselors to gain a working knowledge of these learning styles and to teach students to identify their learning styles so that students might learn how to learn.

Individuals also have a preference for particular learning environments and times of day. Helping students to identify those conditions will promote optimal learning and adaptation to diverse teaching environments and tasks.

SUMMARY

The school counseling program belongs to the stakeholders, and the school counselor actively seeks to identify stakeholder needs using a multitude of potential data sources and time-honored methods for assessing them. Data allows school counselors to target specific needs and populations and to prioritize programming while also assessing the system for barriers to student achievement and well-being. Once school counselors have identified needs, goals, and measurable objectives, research-supported curriculum becomes the focus. Best practices necessitate that school counselors become savvy

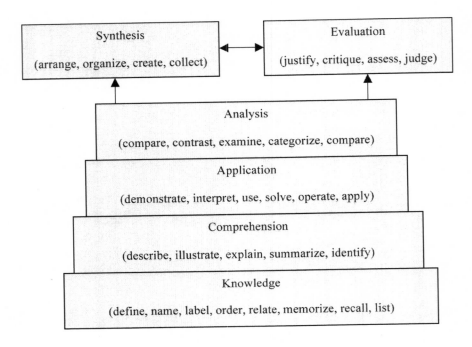

Figure 2.1.   Bloom's taxonomy and associated verbs

consumers of research in order to explore, identify, and apply research-supported prevention and intervention strategies and to create research-based
curriculum. School counselors also apply a working knowledge of learning
styles, learning levels, and multiple intelligences when creating curriculum
that is sensitive to the diverse needs of students.

Chapter Three

Counselor or Educator?

The ASCA, in collaboration with the CACREP, TSCI, and other professional counseling associations, has made great strides in defining contemporary school counseling functions, services, and practices. Unfortunately, vague and inconsistent school counselor roles and responsibilities across states and school divisions continue to strangle the profession's progress.

The strong reaction within the profession to TSCI's switch to an academic-focused paradigm implied a neglect of the counseling role of the school counselor (Guerra, 1998). Some equated this to a change in professional identity—a change that some fear may result in a unilateral identification of the school counselor as educator rather than counselor. This concern is justifiable given the administrative thrust by some schools that encourage school counselors to earn NBPTS's national school counselor certification by offering them salary increases not afforded to those who earn the NBCC national school counselor certification (discussed in chapter 1).

This book promotes the dual roles of educator and counselor, understanding that while counseling is the primary role, it is the role of educator that makes school counselors a special breed: that is what sets them apart from other counseling specialties. This chapter provides a conceptualization and operationalization of these two roles in the context of a comprehensive school counseling program that attends to the whole child and adolescent.

Defining and framing school counselor functions in relation to these roles provides a conceptually sound structure from which to operationalize and authenticate both roles, which can be summarized as follows: school counselors are both counselors and educators who focus on the student as learner, with school counseling services designed, delivered, and documented in an accountable manner that directly and indirectly advances both academic achievement and student development and well-being. Professional progress rests in school counselors' ability to embrace the belief that a healthy mind is essential to a good education. Adept school counselors move fluently between the two roles for optimal student development, all the while documenting the practices that demonstrate the direct, positive impact they have on their students.

School counselors also engage in many shared functions, which include the following: teaming, consulting, informing, collaborating, leading, advocating, counseling, programming, assessing, referring, evaluating, coordinating, and reporting.

The remainder of this chapter is dedicated to operationalizing the school counselor's dual roles. In doing so, the specific functions and activities inherent in each unique role are described.

SCHOOL COUNSELOR: THE ROLE OF COUNSELOR

The CACREP ensures the clinical competence of school counselors by requiring successful completion of eight core counseling competencies. CACREP also ensures the counselor's readiness by requiring a successful matriculation through school counseling specialty competencies, which prepare counselors for their roles as both counselor and educator.

School counselors who believe it is futile to address the academic needs of students in the midst of personal, social, and physical challenges are likely perpetuating student achievement gaps and inequitable access to educational opportunities. Likewise, the fruits of academic-focused school counseling are enjoyed by all students, so the academic-focused school counselor should fully understand how personal, social, emotional, and physical development affects learning and design prevention and intervention programs accordingly.

The contemporary systems-focused model for school counseling does not disregard individual counseling, which remains a mainstay in any comprehensive school counseling program (ASCA, 2012). The problem has been that the traditional mental health model has created an overreliance on individual counseling, which cannot be justified in an age of contemporary school counseling dedicated to systems-focused prevention and intervention in the delivery of both direct and indirect services.

Mental health models conceptualize social-emotional functioning as an end in itself. This explains in part why some K–12 students are in individual school counseling "forever" and why school counseling goals from a mental health perspective are vague and tangential to academic success and learning (Eschenauer & Hayes, 2005, p. 245). For this reason, school counseling alone is not in the best interest of children and adolescents experiencing severe and persistent issues. To provide ongoing counseling sessions with students whose issues cannot be sufficiently addressed solely within the scope of counseling is in violation of professional ethical guidelines. School counselors can best meet the specific mental health needs of these students through a collaborative model that recognizes when students' needs require more specialized skills.

When those skills are needed, school counselors work with other stakeholders to provide optimal and specialized services that place the safety and well-being of children first. School counselors may involve the school psychologist, school social worker, child study team, school nurse, and special education teachers. School counselors may also provide parents with community resources that list but do not specifically endorse any one entity, for example, specialized counselors, psychological and psychiatric services, social services, child-care services, community services boards, spiritual and religious agencies, and support groups.

Because contemporary school counseling emphasizes collaboration, underscoring the need to make appropriate counseling referrals to meet the complex mental health needs of students, counselors can help reduce and even prevent the horrific acts of school violence demonstrated at Columbine, Virginia Tech, and other schools across the nation by remaining diligent in their efforts to identify and encourage familial support and make appropriate referrals for troubled students. Once appropriate referrals are in place, school counselors can implement brief interventions and consult with teachers and parents to provide strategies for implementation at home and in the classroom.

Response to Intervention and Positive Behavioral Support

Although originally conceptualized for students with disabilities, programs such as Response to Intervention (RTI) and Positive Behavioral and Support Interventions (PBSI) can help ensure early identification and intervention for struggling students. RTI and PBSI aid in mediating problematic behaviors, improving academic achievement, reducing the school dropout rate, and creating environments optimal to teaching and learning for all students.

As responsive services, RTI and PBSI are data driven (e.g., discipline records, attendance reports, test scores, course enrollment patterns, special education placement patterns, gifted program placement patterns, graduation rates, and college entrance records) and applied based on need. The core belief of these behavior systems is that some students need more intense or individualized instruction in order to be successful learners.

RTI and PBSI services are as unique as the students, varying in type, intensity, and duration based on level of need and progress toward established educational, career, and personal-social goals. Services may include:

- Dropout prevention and mediating attendance issues
- Decision making and goal setting
- Counseling and behavioral support
- Referral
- Career planning and assessment
- Parenting skills
- Transitioning

School counselors use a multitier approach to align the comprehensive school counseling program with the RTI and PBSI systematically applied processes and use educational and behavioral data to monitor student progress (Schellenberg, 2018). Table 3.1 demonstrates this alignment and the school counselor's responsibility in the RTI process.

Strengths-Based Counseling

Common school counseling responsive services include fostering optimism, cognitive restructuring, problem solving, strengths-based counseling, and promoting developmental assets. School counselors assist students in identifying support systems and their own unique personal attributes to strengthen protective factors and enhance resilience.

Strengths-based counseling interventions that place responsibility for success on the student are educational, empowering, and help to develop coping skills that can be accessed into adulthood. Strengths-based counseling is an emerging positive psychology that accesses inherent strengths to identify student resources and support for addressing the problem and emphasizes the importance of protective factors in combating risk factors and enhancing

Table 3.1. Responses to Intervention in Comprehensive School Counseling.

Program / RTI Process	Role of the School Counselor
Tier 1: Universal core instructional interventions (all students, preventive and proactive)	1. Standards and competencies (foundation) 2. Guidance curriculum (delivery system) 3. Individual student planning (delivery) 4. Curriculum action plan (management) 5. Curriculum results report (accountability)
Tier 2: Supplemental/strategic intervention (students at some risk)	1. Standards and competencies (foundation) 2. Individual student planning (delivery) • Small-group appraisal • Small-group advisement 3. Responsive services (delivery) • Consultation • Individual counseling • Small-group counseling 4. Closing the gap action plan (management) 5. Closing the gap results report (accountability)
Tier 3: Intensive, individual interventions (students at high risk)	1. Standards and competencies (foundation) 2. Responsive services (delivery) • Consultation • Individual counseling • Small-group counseling • Referral to school or community services 3. Closing the gap action plan (management) 4. Closing the gap results report (accountability)

Adapted from 2008 ASCA position statement, response to intervention.

resilience. Current and past successes are considered in addressing future challenges. The approach embraces the philosophy that treatment is not just about fixing what is broken, but nurturing what is best within ourselves, which places resilience building in the realm of not just responsive services but preventative services, using approaches such as classroom guidance (Bardhoshi, Duncan, & Erford, 2017). Lists of development assets for early childhood, middle childhood, and adolescence are made available by the Search Institute (2007) at www.search-institute.org/developmental-assets/ lists. Each list depicts forty developmental assets considered building blocks for healthy development. The following eight categories are included in the lists:

- Support
- Empowerment
- Boundaries and expectations

- Constructive use of time
- Commitment to learning
- Positive values
- Social competencies
- Positive identity

The Invisible Student

Contemporary school counselors are still addressing the clarion call to ensure that we identify and provide services to meet the needs of the "invisible" student (Sink, 2011, p. ii). These are often the students who are not applying themselves to realize their full potential or who are not speaking up to get the assistance needed for optimal mental health and well-being. These students are more introverted, shy, or are quiet and unengaged due to a lack of motivation suffering from personal, social, and emotional issues, usually in silence (Cahill et al., 2018; Dong, Hwang, Shadiev, & Chen, 2017; Flett & Hewitt, 2013; Kerby & Wroughton, 2017; Matteson, 2014; Rosheim, 2018; Sink, 2011). In general, these students just get by academically and appear to be doing just fine, with average grades and no disciplinary problems. This may be the student who doesn't make waves and simply blends in with the crowd (Matteson, 2014; Sink, 2011). The absence of waves, however, could indicate a silent drowning and lost potential, not only for the student but also his family, school, and community.

The invisible student is an unfamiliar focus for school counselors. Although services are provided to all students as part of a comprehensive school counseling program, focused attention is typically given to under-achieving, special needs, at-risk, and advanced-functioning students. For the most part, the invisible student has usually been under the radar, at least until recently.

Strategies for identifying this historically underserved population are needed. Research has provided some insight into strategies that appear to be indicating positive outcomes for these students, such as the use of clickers in the classroom (Dong et al., 2017). These are hand-held devices that allow students to pose questions, answer questions, and even ask to pause the lesson and go back to a specific point, without drawing attention to themselves. Instead of open classroom discussion, or in addition to it, time could also be allotted to write and reflect on the lecture or lesson presented (Rosheim, 2018). Students' attitudes impact learning, engagement, and performance, so assessing their attitudes, not just examining their aggregate scores, would provide information useful to the teacher and the school counselor for early group or individualized intervention (Cahill et al., 2018; Kamarath & Brooker, 2017; Kerby & Wroughton, 2017).

The power of engaged teaching cannot be stressed enough. Teachers must not rely on any single model for lesson delivery as it may overlook the dynamic process of student engagement in a given classroom. Research has demonstrated the value of higher levels of teacher cognitive flexibilities (Stein, Miness, & Kintz, 2018) in promoting higher levels of student engagement. This means that contemporary school counselors will want to learn more about cognitive flexibility theory and the complexities of student engagement, which will provide teachers with professional development opportunities that will demonstrate how data-supported strategies can promote this higher level of student engagement rather than the basic compartmentalized methods of instruction. The creation and revisiting of academic and career plans by way of individual student planning, a requirement of most schools beginning in the middle school years but also taking place as early as elementary school, is one avenue to detecting the invisible student. Delivering the school counseling curriculum by way of classroom guidance lessons, at all levels, would allow the school counselor to observe students, watching for the quiet or disengaged students and meeting with them just to check in and see how they are doing academically, personally, emotionally, and socially. That one contact may be enough to get them moving in the right direction.

The relationship between academic success and personal, emotional, social, and physical well-being is a door that swings both ways. As such, it is important for school counselors to encourage not only the invisible students but all students faced with challenges that may be impacting their learning and the belief in their ability to change, grow, and overcome. School counselors should encourage students to embrace academics as an avenue to a promising, self-directed future while also seeking assistance from the school counselor for issues negatively impacting their life and learning. Academic-focused channeling can be therapeutic, motivational, and build competencies, self-esteem, and psychological resilience—epitomizing the specialty of school counseling. It is important to frame, or reframe in some cases, challenge as our greatest asset, pushing us forward. Standards blending, discussed later in this chapter, exploits this reciprocal relationship for total student development.

In addition to responsive services, school counselors should demonstrate a heightened emphasis on being proactive in anticipating and meeting the personal, social, and emotional health needs of students, as well as engage in purposeful programming designed to remove formidable barriers to academic achievement and well-being for all students.

Spiritual and Religious Development

Contemporary school counseling practices call for school counselors to attend to the spiritual and religious aspects of student development, going so far as to demonstrate how it is their ethical responsibility to do so (Bohecker, Schellenberg, & Silvey, 2017; Briggs, Akos, Czyszczon, & Eldridge, 2011; Gallo, 2014; Kimbel & Schellenberg, 2014).

Once taboo in our schools, this topic is now viewed as our ethical responsibility in meeting the diverse cultural and developmental holistic needs of students. Spiritual and religious development is a critical aspect of human development, a cultural agent, and a natural component for exploration in the counseling process that significantly impacts the student's worldview and the counseling relationship (Briggs et al., 2011; Schellenberg, 2018).

ASCA's Ethical Standards for School Counselors (2016a) states that school counselors "respect students' values, beliefs, and cultural background and do not impose school counselor's personal values on students or their families." The ASCA Ethical Standards also state that the school counselor "acquires educational, consultation and training experiences to improve awareness, knowledge, skills and effectiveness in working with, advocating for, and affirming all students from diverse populations including spiritual/religious identity and appearance." The ASCA School Counselor Competencies (2012) and ASCA Position Statements, however, do not offer guidance as to how school counselors might go about effectively meeting students' spiritual and religious needs.

Uncertain as to how to appropriately address the sensitive topic of spirituality and religion and to address the topic in a manner that would be considered by parents, students, and administrators to be ethical, professional, and legal, school counselors have for the most part avoided the topic. In an effort to promote communications around this crucial topic and provide needed guidance, ASCA devoted an entire special issue in 2004 of its journal, *Professional School Counseling* (PSC), that addressed the spiritual and religious development of students as part of a comprehensive school counseling program.

Much like building multicultural competence, building the competence needed to work with students who hold diverse spiritual and religious beliefs begins with identifying personal biases and committing to learning more about various spiritual and religious practices and how they impact social-emotional, academic, and career decisions (Boheckeret al., 2017; Farmer, 2017; Kimbel & Schellenberg, 2014; Magaldi-Dopman & Park-Taylor, 2014; Sink & Devlin, 2011).

When considering curriculum development for the school counseling program, allow your guiding philosophy to be teaching versus preaching. That is, you should objectively educate about spirituality and religion by (1) being descriptive and unbiased in the information presented, (2) teaching respect and appreciation of diversity, and (3) introducing literature or current events for class discussion that involve spirituality, religion, personal beliefs, and values. As Wolf points out, discussing issues related to spirituality is both constitutional and ethical in accordance with the First Amendment of the Constitution and the ASCA Code of Ethics, respectively.

In part, the key to maintaining objectivity while teaching on topics related to spirituality and religion begins with an understanding of the differences between the two. Religion is an organized practice that generally involves specific beliefs, ritualized worship, and an establishment such as a church, while spirituality is generally broader, unstructured, and focused on the individual's essence of being in relation to nature and the universe, and it may or may not include religion (Schellenberg, 2018).

In addition to spiritual and religious sensitivity in individual and group counseling and school counseling core curriculum development, school counselors might also support student spirituality and religious beliefs through development assets and character education (Dobmeier, 2011). School counselors might consider participating in student-initiated spiritual and religious events such as the annual "See You at the Pole" prayer meeting. Section 9524 of the Elementary and Secondary Education Act (ESEA) constitutionally protects prayer in public schools (U.S. Department of Education, 2004) and school counselors who explore issues of spirituality with students are engaging in both ethically responsible and culturally competent counseling practices (Schellenberg, 2018).

To offer school counselors guidelines for professional practice, the following Spiritual and Religious Competencies for School Counselors (referred to hereafter as *guidelines*) and approaches and strategies for meeting the spiritual and religious needs of students are provided (Bohecker et al., 2017; Kimbel & Schellenberg, 2014). These guidelines includes twenty competencies within five domains that are grounded in school counseling research and literature as well as professional standards and ethical codes. The first four domains are adapted from the culture and worldview, counselor self-awareness, human and spiritual development, and assessment domains. The final domain of the Spiritual and Religious Competencies for School Counselors aligns with the delivery component of the ASCA National Model (2012), as school counselors spend a significant amount of time providing direct and indirect services to address this component compared to responsibilities related to the other three components (i.e., foundation, management, and accountability). In fact, the delivery component of the ASCA National Model accounts for 80 percent of the school counselor's use of time (ASCA, 2012). For this reason, approaches and techniques for practical application in the delivery of direct and indirect student services are suggested below:

School Counseling Core Curriculum

- Make use of spiritual and religious documents and books, including religious or "holy" books, during classroom instruction to teach civic values, virtues, and moral conduct.
- Explore with students the ways in which they can meet goals and reach potential with good values, virtues, and moral conduct.
- Include religious and spiritual careers as options during career exploration curriculum delivery.
- Teach spiritual and religious beliefs and associated holidays during curriculum delivery.
- Implement school-wide programs that promote peer interactions, an appreciation of differences, and a climate where the peaceful resolution of problems is encouraged (e.g., peer mediation, conflict resolution, peer transition, new student orientation, tutoring).
- Engage students in developmentally appropriate discussions about current news and world reports and the role of moral conduct with regard to the events presented.
- Hang a poster in the school counseling office with a multitude of spiritual systems and religions represented.

Individual Student Planning

- Include volunteer work at food banks and homeless shelters in academic and career plans.

- Provide students with a list of community service agencies that include spiritual and religious organizations and activities.

Responsive Services

- Make use of bibliotherapy to illustrate exemplary moral behavior.
- Have students engage in role-plays that are rich in opportunities to develop empathy, demonstrate respect for others, and work through issues laden with spiritual and religious themes.
- Explore case studies to encourage reflection and reasoning as well as to highlight ways in which the case might be resolved using moral decision making and positive social interactions.

Referrals

- Develop a list of community resources for students and parents for career (e.g., employment and inventory websites) and academic support (e.g., tutoring, test preparation), as well as intervention for mental health issues (e.g., suicide ideation, eating disorders, depression). Include common spiritual and religious institutions and the services provided.
- Create comprehensive lists of common spiritual and religious belief systems and inform parents that you have such resources available.

Collaboration and Consultation

- Team with teachers to sponsor student-led spiritual and religious clubs.
- Team with teachers to conduct school-wide character education activities and recognitions, including morning announcements that emphasize a monthly virtue (e.g., perseverance, courage, truthfulness, kindness, patience, hope, humility).
- Partner with teachers to attend student-sponsored events before and after school such as the annual "See You at the Pole" meeting to model the importance placed on religious and spiritual values and beliefs in schools and communities.
- Conduct parent workshops on parenting styles and enlist objective research that speaks to the introduction of values and beliefs in relation to early child development and well-being.
- Conduct parent-teacher workshops on the impact of belief and values systems in relation to school violence and school climate as presented in

the research (e.g., examine belief and value systems of differing countries and the prevalence of school violence).

- Partner with parents, teachers, and the community to coordinate stamp-out-violence activities that foster awareness and promote peaceable schools.
- Team with teachers and administrators to develop school mottos that revolve around the fair and equal treatment of all people and appreciation of differences.
- Work with parents and community agencies to coordinate an annual outdoor around-the-world-day whereby all countries are represented, highlighting customs that include cuisine, clothing, spiritual and religious beliefs, and more.

Peer Programming

Students helping students is one of a school counselor's most valuable resources. Research to support the positive outcomes of peer-to-peer support programs is well documented (Goodrich, 2018; McLeod, Jones, & Cramer, 2015). Peer helping programs are also encouraged by ASCA, with ethical guidelines established to ensure that student welfare is safeguarded, emphasizing the importance of proper training and supervision of peer helpers by school counselors (ASCA, 2016a).

Peer-to-peer programs might include transition buddies, orientation programs, peer tutoring, peer relationships, and peer mediation (Goodrich, 2018; McLeod et al., 2015). Chapter 4 provides an effective example of a school-wide peer mediation program and evaluation that identifies, targets, and reduces school violence, an obstacle to academic achievement and the personal, social, and emotional well-being of students (Schellenberg, Parks-Savage, & Rehfuss, 2007). The program studied establishes the need for school-wide peer mediation programs and reveals the link between peer mediation programs and academic achievement. The study documents research and literature that emphasize the detrimental effects of aggressive student interactions on the school's culture, learning environment, and academic productivity.

Proactive Change Agents

Proactive approaches to meeting the needs of students may require that school counselors position themselves in ways that increase visibility, which aids in enhancing school climate; fosters relationships with students, parents, teachers, and principals; and identifies at-risk students (i.e., withdrawn, flat affect, socially inept, overly aggressive, visibly distressed). For example, school counselors may greet students in main hallways prior to the start of morning classes and at the end of the school day. School counselors might consider frequent visits to the cafeteria to give out bookmarks that contain useful information such as study and test-taking tips, important dates, names of school counselors, counseling department services and website, and career exploration resources and access codes. In addition, promoting the open-door policy, conveying an approachable demeanor, and maintaining a welcoming office (e.g., chair facing the door vs. back to the door) encourages interaction.

Many adults and students who experience distress do not actively seek out support (Auger, 2004), and many stakeholders simply cannot find the time to make an appointment to meet with the school counselor. As such, it is important that school counselors be creative in getting meaningful information to stakeholders for sound decision making and problem solving (Kennedy & Stanley, 2015; Shimoni & Greenberger, 2015). Information and resources might include crises response, support programs, parenting programs, tutoring contacts, substance use and abuse, eating disorders, counseling services available to students, study skills, test-taking strategies, organizational and time-management skills, problem solving and conflict resolution, communication skills, and information that describes what to look for in determining the need for counseling services.

Establishing or tapping into a school-based Parent-Teacher-Student Resource Center (PTSRC) as an avenue for information dissemination is essential to meeting the needs of all stakeholders. PTSRCs are efficient mediums for promoting student development in a way that accommodates diverse schedules and is also an excellent way to get parents involved.

As Moles (1993) points out, there are many parents who want very much to get involved in the local school community but for a variety of reasons do not step forward. Extend an invitation to parents and be specific about the assistance and hours for which they are being recruited—watch what happens!

Parent volunteers are often an untapped resource in schools where human resources are generally limited. Parent volunteers can oversee daily PTSRC operations, providing assistance and direction to stakeholders seeking specific information, coordinating requests for information, and maintaining informational flow.

Websites, too, are an expedient way to pass valuable information to stakeholders. Websites have been found to be an effective and cost-effective medium for providing information and making resources available to stakeholders (Kennedy & Stanley, 2015; Shimoni & Greenberger, 2015). Information and resources listed on school counseling websites can enhance student development and well-being and support healthy schools, homes, and communities. It is most imperative, however, that school counselors understand that not every family has a computer or access to the internet. Websites can therefore not be the only means for information dissemination to important others.

School counselors are dogmatic in seeking to meet the mental health needs of students. By applying these constructs, school counselors are practicing from a contemporary perspective that expands services and promotes a more proactive and collaborative approach to meeting students' personal, social, emotional, and physical needs. Contemporary practices necessitate that school counselors exercise the counselor role as a part of fulfilling the educator role— the role that sets counseling in the schools apart from other counseling specialties and defines it.

SCHOOL COUNSELOR: THE ROLE OF EDUCATOR

Education and training that distinguish the school counselor as an educator involves pre-K–12 program design and delivery, classroom instruction, theories of learning, child and adolescent development, standardized testing and assessment, use of technology, behavioral theory, disability and exceptional behavior, identification of student competencies and ways to achieve academic competency, identification and removal of barriers to academic achievement, developing effective learning environments, needs assessment, and educational program evaluation. Because the role of educator involves instruction, a few states still require a teaching background in order to become a school counselor despite research that disproves such suppositions. Therefore, it is important that this book speak to the research in this area of continued debate—a debate that was deepened with the NBPTS's establishment of an advanced voluntary "teacher" certification for school counselors (discussed in chapter 1), perpetuating the blurred roles of teacher and school counselor.

Research has examined the question of whether school counselors should be teachers prior to becoming school counselors. These studies indicate that school administrators and school counselor supervisors deem school counselors without teaching experience to be as effective as those with teaching experience. In some cases, the majority of school counselors without teaching experience were unexpectedly found to be more effective in their overall performance than those with teaching experience (Beale, 1995; Dilley, Foster, & Bowers, 1973; Olson & Allen, 1993).

One landmark study conducted during the crux of the debate provides evidence that having served as a teacher results in a multitude of poor counseling habits (Arbuckle, 1961). The implications of this study are significant, albeit aged, indicating a need for counselor educators to work closely with former teachers to extinguish most of what they had learned as teachers in order to become effective school counselors.

Arbuckle's (1961) findings are further supported in a more recent study of the personal and professional adjustments of school counseling interns with and without teaching experience. The study, conducted by Peterson, Goodman, Keller, and McCauley (2004), indicates that former teachers face unique challenges that threatened a successful transition into the school counseling profession. Although it appears to have been established that teaching experience does not equal effective school counseling, there is general agreement that instructional skills are helpful in a profession that is expected to provide instruction. Therefore, counselor educators are diligent in their efforts to ensure the instructional competency of preservice school counselors in course curriculum and in the practice setting during counselor education programs.

In addition to the formal course work noted earlier in this chapter, counselor educators must also demonstrate instructional competencies with diverse populations during classroom experiential learning activities and internships. Preservice school counselors are also required to demonstrate knowledge of the pre-K–12 curriculum and engage in practicum and internship experiences throughout the counselor education program. Preservice school counselors therefore have multiple opportunities to enhance their knowledge of curriculum development, collaborate with teachers, and develop classroom management and instructional skills while also gaining a familiarity with the school setting.

Counselor education programs prepare school counselors for their role of educator by emphasizing the alignment of school counseling activities with academic achievement. They also accentuate the need to optimize the instructional competency and classroom management skills of school counselors. Training is therefore provided in instructional strategies, academic achievement, learning theory, multiple intelligences, and classroom management.

School counselors in training who wish to engage in supplemental learning are encouraged to engage in job shadowing, interviewing, and dialoguing with currently practicing school counselors. School counselors in training in the practice setting can improve in the areas noted by reviewing relevant journal articles and participating in instructional planning, conferences, and workshops.

Instruction is but one function inherent in the school counselor's role of educator: they are also required to apply academic standards, interpret standardized testing score reports, engage in standardized testing programs, develop research-supported curriculum, and create and evaluate needs- and standards-based educational programs. Using their well-defined collaborative and consultative skills, school counselors also work with teachers to modify the classroom climate for optimal learning. Together, they identify systemic areas of academic deficits and specific low-achieving student populations for intervention. School counselors then tailor programming to target students' specific academic needs while simultaneously meeting the personal, social, and career development needs of students.

STANDARDS BLENDING

Aligning School Counseling with Academic Achievement

Leaders in education and school counseling agree that implementation of standards-based programs that align school counseling with academic achievement missions are considered best practices for school counselors. Alignment approaches are needed that provide school counselors with a direct path for increasing academic achievement and closing the achievement gap.

Until recently, alignment approaches that integrate academic standards and school counseling standards, such as the Mindsets and Behaviors for Student Success (ASCA, 2014), have been random, spur-of-the-moment, superfluous, or absent from school counseling programming. This chapter introduces standards blending as a specific and unified cross-walking approach for inclusion as a deliberate, inveterate, and integral component of a comprehensive school counseling program. ASCA expects school counselors to blend their 2014 standards with other appropriate standards. The paragraphs that follow demonstrate how so-called standards blending can be implemented and assimilated as a permanent programming strategy for improving academic achievement.

Standards blending is a systems-focused, integrative, and student-centered cross-walking approach that directly and overtly aligns school counseling programs with academic achievement missions. School counselors methodically identify and blend specific core academic standards with school counseling standards for integrated lessons that assist students in making connections to real life and across curricula. As a primary and anchored appendage to a comprehensive developmental school counseling program, standards blending is the embodiment of academic- and systems-focused practices.

Standards blending does not replace the counselor role, nor was it meant as an approach to address every unique issue within a school. The approach requires school counselors to make use of their skills as both educators and counselors, integrating both the Mindsets and Behaviors and other core academic standards. This cross-walking method allows the school counselor to meet the career, academic, and social-emotional development needs of students while demonstrating a direct impact on academic achievement.

School counselors may wish to blend all core academic standards with the Mindsets and Behaviors standards to create the alignment. It is recommended, however, that language arts and mathematics standards be the focus of standards blending because reading, writing, and arithmetic have always been basic to schooling and to building a solid foundation from which to learn other core subjects. These subject areas are also those most prized by potential employers.

The unrelenting call for accountability in educational practices and standards-based educational reform has heightened the importance of rigorous, evidence-based practices. Standards blending is grounded in these nationally accepted standards that are influenced by research and knowledge in the field.

In addition to a sound standards base, perception, process, and outcome data are collected to assess the meaningfulness of standards blending, and several studies validate its effectiveness (Schellenberg, 2007; Schellenberg & Grothaus, 2009, 2011). These studies depict the usefulness of standards blending for the delivery of core school counseling curriculum, individual student planning, and responsive services at both the elementary and secondary levels with varying populations (e.g., ethnicity, special needs, advanced functioning). Research in the application of standards blending has consistently resulted in improved academic performance in mathematics and language arts, as well as the personal, social, and career development of students.

Standards blending promotes the application of differential instruction, assessing student needs, accommodating unique student learning profiles, and considering student readiness and interests in curriculum planning and delivery. Standards blending also promotes multiple learning categories (i.e., cognitive, affective, and psychomotor) and the six levels of learning of Bloom's Taxonomy (Bloom, 1953): knowledge, comprehension, application, analysis, synthesis, and evaluation. As a holistic and constructivist approach, standards blending is an instructional strategy that is compatible with brain-based learning.

Standards blending encourages students to draw upon previous knowledge, make connections, get involved, explore, discuss, discover, and personalize the content. This approach is pragmatic, providing students with a method by which to improve comprehension by connecting curricula and visualizing the interrelationships of learning and real life. Students socially interact with the curriculum, fellow students, and teachers in small learning communities where information is processed and problems are examined, deconstructed, and resolved. Approaches such as these have been linked to the development of background knowledge, intrinsic interest, and higher-order intelligence, as well as greater academic achievement and a heightened motivation toward learning (Marzano, 2004; Sink, 2005; Vansteenkiste, Lens, & Deci, 2006).

Blending academic standards and school counseling Mindsets and Behaviors competencies requires a working knowledge of school counseling and academic standards as well as consultation with the classroom teacher to coordinate the pacing of lessons. Most schools offer pacing guides that outline the timing of classroom instruction that addresses specific academic standards.

Standards blending can be delivered as an indirect service by teaming and partnering with teachers and parents to teach the cross-walking approach for use in the regular education classroom with a variety of subjects or outside of school in daily parent-child interactions and activities. Curriculum that includes the standards blending approach generally includes the school counseling core curriculum and responsive services, namely classroom lessons and small-group programs, respectively.

Consider the following case for illustration of the delivery of core school counseling curriculum in a classroom or small-group session using standards blending. The lesson blends both Mindsets and Behaviors developmentally appropriate for eighth-grade students as well as the mathematics and language arts core academic standards. Note the differential instructional components in the lesson's design and activities and the inclusion of the three domains and six levels of learning of Bloom's Taxonomy.

The school counselor is preparing to deliver core school counseling curriculum or a small-group session to eighth-grade students that addresses the Mindsets and Behaviors for Student Success deemed appropriate for a comprehensive school counseling program and as indicated by a needs assessment conducted at the start of the school year. The school's academic pacing guide or eighth-grade teacher indicates that the eighth-grade English teachers are working on oral language development with the students in March, specifically interviewing techniques to gain information—or this was identified as a need for a specific group of students, in which case small-group counseling may be conducted.

In addition to the Mindsets and Behaviors competency, school counselors incorporate the language arts standards being addressed at that time. The lesson curriculum includes a discussion of the importance of researching different careers to locate, evaluate, and interpret career and educational information (Mindsets and Behaviors career development competency). Informational interviews are defined and discussed to include students' thoughts and feelings associated with the career exploration process and conducting informational interviews. Students are asked to give examples of the value and different uses of informational interviews and how they compare to other methods used in the past for the collection of information. Students are also asked to conduct an informational interview (language arts competency) for the purpose of career exploration (Mindsets and Behaviors career competency). Individually, students prepare ten relevant questions for the interview (language arts competency). Students role-play the interview with the school counselor and each other, asking the questions they prepared (language arts competency) and noting the responses (language arts competency). Together, the class evaluates the effectiveness of the interviews in learning more about career choices (both language arts and Mindsets and Behaviors competency).

Math standards being addressed by teachers at the present time include estimations, data analysis and conjectures, and identifying the mean of a data set. Therefore, the school counselor requires that at least five questions involve proportions such as scaling questions (e.g., how would you rate your job satisfaction on a scale of one to ten?). Students are required to represent scaled responses using a table or graph and then analyze patterns, relationships, and similarities within their data set and differences between each other's data sets. Together, the group develops inferences about their findings (language arts, mathematics, and Mindsets and Behaviors competencies).

The school counselor closes the lesson with an appraisal of the informational interview specific to career exploration. Students also judge the applicability and usefulness of informational interviews in other areas of their personal, academic, and professional lives. Again, the school counselor assesses students' thoughts and feelings associated with the career exploration process and conducting informational interviews.

The eighth-grade lesson noted above can also be tailored to meet the developmental and educational needs of high school students. This school counseling lesson or small-group activity applied to ninth-, tenth-, eleventh-, and twelfth-grade students meets the Mindsets and Behaviors career development competencies as well as language arts (e.g., communication skills and strategies, evaluating data, developing research skills, application of language skills) and mathematics standards (e.g., number and operations; measurement; data analysis and probability; developing and evaluating inferences and predictions based on data; and mathematical communication, connections, and representation).

Closing the Achievement Gap

Contemporary school counseling continues its emphasis on closing achievement gaps and promoting equitable access and attainment by disaggregating data and identifying existing subgroup discrepancies. School counselors are then challenged to design approaches that assist in closing any gaps in order to demonstrate adequate yearly progress and equality in the distribution of services. National data have identified academic achievement gaps between low-income and minority students and their more affluent peers, students with disabilities and nondisabled students, and between males and females. Therefore, once school counselors, in collaboration with school administrators and teachers, have identified low-achieving subgroups in a particular school or district, research-supported and standards-based programming should be designed to aid in closing achievement gaps.

School counselors can design small-group curriculum, for example, to specifically target areas of academic weaknesses. Low-achieving students often experience multiple precipitating issues and stressors that frequently go unrecognized and untreated, placing these students at risk for school failure. Using standards blending, school counselors can address the mental health needs of these students, building personal, social, and emotional well-being and resilience while simultaneously and directly addressing targeted academic needs.

Consider the following lesson for illustration of a small-group curriculum that provides at-risk students with both remediation and reinforcement in language arts and mathematics in addition to social skills development by way of standards blending. Again, note in the lesson's design differential instruction strategies and the inclusion of Bloom's three domains and six levels of learning.

A teacher refers Topeka, a third-grade student, to the school counselor for a social skills small-group intervention. Consultation with the teacher and a review of Topeka's class work and formal assessments reveal difficulty in math, particularly with numbers and number sense such as the concepts of greater than, less than, and equal to; parts of sets; and fractions. As a result of school counselor–teacher consultation, the school counselor addresses areas of weakness in mathematics while also defining, identifying, experiencing, and appraising the concepts of sharing and fairness in the social skills group using role-plays and social skills scenarios (language arts and Mindsets and Behaviors competencies).

The school counselor gives Topeka twenty social skills scenario cards and asks her to give herself and each student an equal number of cards (mathematics competencies). After Topeka has passed out all the cards, the school counselor counts the cards in front of each of the four students and initiates discussions that connect the concepts of sharing, fairness, sets, greater than, less than, and fractions. The cards, students, and role-plays are manipulated in order to visualize the relationships, create predictions, and assess the value of the language arts, mathematics, and social skills concepts presented.

The school counselor encourages storytelling (language arts, mathematics, and Mindsets and Behaviors competencies) to relate learning to individual student experiences, needs, and relationships—to life—and to ensure students' understanding of the information presented. Throughout the group lessons, each student's academic areas of weakness are addressed using differential instruction based on specific core academic standards.

The small group presented above is designed to enhance total student development by targeting social, emotional, and academic areas to meet the specific needs of each student in the group. The school counselor addresses multiple areas of language arts and social skills while also providing students with remediation in targeted areas of mathematics. The school counselor also reinforces a variety of grade-level appropriate mathematical concepts for all students.

In addition to the benefits to students, standards blending encourages consulting and teaming with teachers. An atmosphere of collaboration with teachers to accomplish student academic achievement goals has the potential to enhance the teacher–school counselor relationship and strengthen universal achievement.

SUMMARY

Implementation of the school counselor's dual roles of educator and counselor and the functions inherent in each role are fundamental to the continued growth and unification of the profession. The school counselor as counselor meets the social and emotional needs of students within the scope of school counseling. This requires collaboration with professionals within and outside of the school system and the involvement and support of school administrators. The school counselor as educator identifies and removes barriers to academic achievement and, moreover, directly impacts academic achievement through well-planned instructional programming and a working knowledge of academic standards.

The school counselor adeptly combines the roles of educator and counselor using standards blending as a cross-walking approach that integrates academic standards and the Mindsets and Behaviors for Student Success competencies. Standards blending can also be used as a strategy for closing the achievement gap. The school counselor applies differential instructional philosophies with the constructs of Bloom's Taxonomy for creating optimal and individualized curriculum and learning environments.

Chapter Four

Our Bread and Butter

Research and Program Evaluation

Chapter 2 discussed how school counselors identify best practices gleaned from research to support curriculum content and systemic services delivery. During program planning, school counselors identify measurable objectives and assess the program's effectiveness toward meeting those objectives using process, perception, and outcome data. In this regard, school counselors are delivering empirically validated programs that are both data driven and data producing.

Program evaluation is a type of applied research and is the most widely used in schools. It is invaluable in the educational setting where true experiments are extremely difficult due to many uncontrollable variables and the ethical concerns of randomly assigning children and adolescents to treatment conditions and control groups. Program evaluation is an essential competency, legislative mandate, and ethical responsibility of school counselors because they are obligated to systematically collect and analyze data to ensure the continuous improvement of their programming and determine the usefulness of their services in meeting the needs of stakeholders.

ASCA's Ethical Standards for School Counselors (2016a) emphasizes the use of appropriate research and report findings in ways acceptable to the practice of educational and psychological research. The standards further advocate the anonymity of student identity when using data for research or systematic evaluation of school counseling programs.

Often in school counseling circles, just the mention of data elicits a negative response, but as the tide of accountability grows, so too will the demand for data. Routinely gathering, examining, and generating data may help school counselors overcome their aversion to data while demonstrating reflective, investigative, and accountable practices. Facilitating empirically supported school counseling activities, after all, can forever change the direction of a student's life.

Research and program evaluation are empowering and powerful proactive strategies that are necessary to:

- Identify practices that contribute to academic success and the social, emotional, and career development of students
- Develop empirically supported curriculum
- Engage in professional advocacy
- Provide reliable consultation services
- Make programming decisions
- Enhance accountability
- Shape policy in the schools and at the local, state, and federal levels
- Inform and sustain the profession
- Justify funding and resource allocations
- Assess the value of programming and practices

It is important to understand that the analysis of data for program planning and program evaluation does not equal accountability: It is a means by which to demonstrate accountable professional practices, which also include prevention and intervention programming that is supported by standards and services that are professionally, developmentally, ethically, legally, and culturally sound and justifiable.

Program evaluation demonstrates evidence over effort and answers the more critical question "How are students different as a result of school counseling programs?" It is important that program evaluation become an integral component of the school counseling program's research, review, and feedback structure. Research and program evaluation are the school counselor's bread and butter—they sustain us as a profession.

The call for program evaluation in school counseling and for collaborative research conducted by practitioners and counselor educators is still growing (ASCA, 2012, 2014; Schellenberg, 2018; Sink, 2018). Research partnerships benefit both counselor educators and school counseling practitioners. Collaborative studies provide counselor-educators with an opportunity to stay apprised of rapidly changing practice needs for the contemporary school setting and to become involved in applied research in the school setting. Research partnerships with counselor-educators provide school counselors with the opportunity to stay abreast of major developments in school counselor preparation, to target professional development activities, and to develop program evaluation skills and comfort levels with data collection, analysis, and reporting.

PROCESS AND OUTCOME EVALUATION

The following two types of program evaluation, process and outcome, are not to be confused with the three types of data described in chapter 2 as process, perception, and outcome data. Both process and outcome evaluation designs could potentially make use of all three types of the data discussed earlier in this text.

Program evaluations that measure outcome, that is, the effectiveness of the program in achieving intended goals, are important to establish a causal link between school counseling programs and student change, particularly academic achievement. Outcome evaluations, sometimes referred to as summative evaluations or quantitative evaluations, seek to answer the significant question "Did it work?"

Process evaluations, on the other hand, examine program functioning, strengths, weaknesses, and the extent to which the program meets the expectations of and serves the target population. Also known as formative evaluations and qualitative evaluations, they are useful for program decision making and program improvement. Process evaluations seek to answer such questions as "How did it work?" and "How or with what population did it work best?"

School counselors are wise to consider conducting program evaluations that include both measures. Even when outcome measures are positive, additional program data might provide knowledge that can be used to strengthen program outcomes, uncover further needs and unexpected benefits of the program, and identify additional target populations.

PROXIMAL AND DISTAL EVALUATIONS

Proximal evaluation measures are those that take place immediately before and after the program or intervention. Proximal evaluations allow school counselors to establish correlations and, in some cases (depending on the strength of the research design), a causal link between school counseling interventions and outcomes. Proximal evaluation can demonstrate that school counselor programming is, indeed, making a positive difference in the lives of students. Understandably, measures that take place immediately before and after an intervention can claim with some degree of certainty that it was that intervention that caused the change. For this reason, proximal evaluation is the most pungent type of evaluation in a climate where school counselors need to demonstrate their worth as both counselors and educators.

Distal evaluations, on the other hand, are measures taken at some point not immediately after the intervention and can be multiple measures taken over time—sometimes called repeated measures. Distal measures alone do not have the power to provide strong correlations or a definitive link to school counseling programming due to the great number of factors (i.e., extraneous variables) that impact student development over time (i.e., between phases of evaluation). They do, however, have the advantage of demonstrating that the change that took place initially (proximal measure) has remained (or not) and for how long. Distal evaluations are often used as a means of cross validation to either further support or call into question proximal evaluation outcomes and to offer insights into program strengths and weaknesses for ongoing improvement (Schellenberg, 2018).

There has been some debate previously over the significance of proximal (immediate) versus distal (long-term) evaluation in linking school counseling services to what students know and can do as a result of the program. There is now consensus that proximal evaluation is necessary, while distal evaluation is nice but not essential. Most believe, however, that both are needed to demonstrate not just change but lasting change attributable to school counseling programming and services.

That said, contemporary school counselors are still being called on to provide clear outcome data that demonstrates enhanced academic achievement and holistic student development that is clearly a result of school counseling programming. So if one must be pitted against the other, then proximal evaluations that collect perception, process, and outcome data are the professional zeitgeist.

Over time, consistent program evaluation will aid school counselors in building a strong knowledge foundation from which to expand, enhance, and tailor procedures and programming to the specific needs of a school division. This knowledge structure will allow school counselors and administrators to make declarative statements about the contributions of school counseling and future directions for school counseling programming.

METHODOLOGY

Program evaluation is a type of field-based outcome study, or, as mentioned previously, a type of action or applied research. There are an infinite number of other types of outcome research designs that could be used to measure any number of research questions. Three of the most commonly used by school counselors in the school setting are nonexperimental, quasi-experimental, and true experimental (Schellenberg, 2018). In short, the true experimental design is the strongest for establishing cause and effect, using random sampling and control groups. The quasi-experimental design does not use random assignment and involves multiple groups or multiple measures. Nonexperimental designs are generally one-time surveys and single observations that have the least value for determining cause and effect between an intervention and outcome.

Pre- and postprogram instruments are the most widely used method of program evaluation, particularly in the schools. Methods may include behavioral observations, rating scales, student portfolios, and curriculum content instruments containing forced-choice items (e.g., multiple choice, true or false, Likert scale) for quantitative analysis.

Program evaluations that use triangulation (i.e., the incorporation of multiple sources of data) strengthen confidence in observed changes. For the same reason, statistical analysis is encouraged using paired sample t-tests for pre- and postprogram data in addition to descriptive statistics such as percentages, categories, counts, and frequencies. An analysis of variance (ANOVA) is suggested for analyzing multiple observations, but attention must be given to statistical assumptions when using an ANOVA and the MANOVA (multivariate analysis of variance).

The example below illustrates evaluation questions, data sources, and methods of data analysis of a comprehensive program evaluation conducted by a school counselor in collaboration with counselor educators (Schellenberg et al., 2007). The evaluation includes both proximal and distal evaluation, process and outcome measures, and the use of multiple data sources for triangulation.

REDUCING LEVELS OF ELEMENTARY SCHOOL VIOLENCE WITH PEER MEDIATION: EVALUATION QUESTIONS, DATA SOURCES, AND METHODS OF DATA ANALYSIS

- Does student knowledge pertaining to conflict, conflict resolution, and mediation increase as a result of Peace Pal training? (Data source: Pre- and post-training questionnaires developed from curriculum and administered prior to training, immediately following training, and three months later; Data analysis: Repeated Measures 1x3 ANOVA)
- Do peer mediation sessions result in the successful resolution of student conflict? (Data source: Peer mediation session records over one academic year; Data analysis: Percentages)
- Do the number of school-wide out-of-school suspensions decrease with the implementation of the Peace Pal program? (Data source: Out-of-school suspension data over a five-year period; Data analysis: Frequencies and percentages)
- Do students who participate in peer mediation sessions view the sessions as valuable? (Data source: Peer mediation session records over one academic year; Data analysis: Percentages)
- Do peer mediators perceive the Peace Pal program as valuable? (Data source: Process questions five years postprogram; Data analysis: Percentages and qualitative)

Evaluation questions were derived from the goal and objectives of the program and were adapted from Schellenberg et al., 2007.

ETHICAL AND LEGAL CONSIDERATIONS

It is important for school counselors to consider the ethical and legal issues associated with conducting research in the schools. Issues to consider include obtaining parental and student informed consent, confidentiality of assessment data, culture and gender bias in the selection of measures, withholding treatment, and the treatment of all students in experimental groups. In addition to a review of the ACA's Code of Ethics and Standards of Practice (2005) and ASCA's Ethical Standards for School Counselors (2016a), the following resources are beneficial when conducting studies in the public school setting: "Competencies in Assessment and Evaluation for School Counselors" (Association for Assessment in Counseling and Education, 1998); Counseling and Educational Research (Houser, 1998); Guiding Principles for Evaluators (American Evaluation Association, 1994); and Program Evaluation: Methods and Case Studies (Posavac & Carey, 2003).

SUMMARY

It is the school counselor's professional and ethical responsibility to demonstrate, document, and promote accountable practices using research and program evaluation. Practitioner and educator-practitioner research is needed that clearly depicts both the immediate and long-term impact of school counseling prevention and intervention activities on student development in general and on student academic achievement in particular.

Both proximal and distal evaluations have their value. Proximal evaluation, however, is necessary to establishing correlational, if not causal, relationships between school counseling programming and student outcomes. While outcome-based evaluations are the priority in school counseling practices, process evaluations have value as well, suggesting the application of a mixed-method approach. Regardless of the type of research and program evaluation conducted, school counselors need to be aware of the ethical and legal issues associated with conducting research in the school setting.

Chapter Five

The Quintessential Contemporary School Counselor

The journey to becoming the quintessential contemporary school counselor begins with a rigorous preparation program that is, preferably, CACREP-accredited and thereby guided by standards and best practices. Formal education in the principles of counseling establishes a critical solid foundation, but much of what the school counselor learns takes place during practice through visionary leadership, sound clinical supervision, continuous self-reflection, ongoing professional development, school counseling association memberships, and networking with others in the profession.

COUNSELOR EDUCATORS

Counselor educators create and shape the attitude, knowledge, skills, and abilities that school counselors bring to the practice setting. Using a variety of educational and instructional philosophies, models, and techniques, counselor educators prepare preservice school counselors to practice in a profession that continues to grow at dizzying rates. They apply a variety of approaches to cover the breadth of knowledge and skills necessary for the preparation of counselors in general and school counselors in particular (Brigman, Villares, & Webb, 2017; Watkinson, Goodman-Scott, Martin, & Biles, 2018).

Like administrators, teachers, and other specialties in pre-K–12 schools, counselor educators understand that accountability has taken permanent residence in school counseling. As such, counselor educators impress upon future school counselors the importance of accountable programming on a daily basis—not just once in a while. Counselor-educator mentoring in program evaluation and the use of data has been found to not only increase preservice school counselors' efficacy in the use of data but also to foster a more positive attitude about accountability (Milsom & McCormick, 2016).

Meeting the challenges of contemporary school counseling necessitates that counselor educators teach the realities of current practices while also ensuring school counselors understand what a comprehensive developmentally appropriate school counseling program should look like in accordance with the ASCA National Model (ASCA, 2012, 2016b). Teaching and demonstrating effective leadership that encompasses both leadership styles and models is essential to developing the quintessential contemporary school counselor (Kneale, Young & Dollarhide, 2017; Michel, Lorelle, & Atkins, 2017).

PEDAGOGY

Due to the traditional mental health–focused pedagogy for school counseling, counselor educators are well experienced and adept in providing clinical instruction that stresses the application of counseling theory and counseling techniques, particularly as it applies to minors, as well as the legal and ethical considerations of counseling practices in the school setting. Counselor-educator expertise in this area is indispensable to clinical competency and the ability of the school counselor to practice skillfully in the role of counselor for children and adolescents.

It is important, however, for counselor educators to ensure that preservice school counselors understand the scope of school counseling practices, specifically regarding mental health–related services to students. Ensuring that preservice school counselors can 1) distinguish between appropriate and inappropriate services with regard to what is considered to be within the scope of school counseling practices and 2) understand situations in which collaboration, consultation, and referral within and outside of the school are necessary is vital to the development, well-being, and safety of children and makes for an accountable practitioner.

Counselor educators who introduce the national common core and state-specific academic content standards in addition to ASCA's Mindsets and Behaviors for Student Success are preparing preservice school counselors to meet the expectations of school administrators, who seek out school counselors capable of cross-walking curriculum to aid in the academic achievement mission. Requiring preservice school counselors to apply both sets of standards, differential instruction, classroom management approaches, and Bloom's constructs in the planning and delivery of classroom guidance lessons provides opportunities to practice and build necessary skills in these areas. Additionally, having preservice school counselors apply strategies using diverse student populations, topics, and group sizes reflects the realities of contemporary practice in a culturally pluralistic educational system.

Teaching standards blending as a part of comprehensive school counseling models such as the ASCA's National Model (2012, 2016b) provides preservice school counselors with a solid foundation and framework from which to build an integrative, academic-focused program that meets the holistic needs of students and that school administrators can readily support. Standards blending is also an excellent approach used by counselor educators to meet CACREP specialty school counseling standards and various state competency requirements for school counselor licensure.

Readying the preservice school counselor for core school counseling curriculum delivery necessitates counselor-educator encouragement of education and training related to instructional skills. Counselor educators incorporate curriculum development, instructional strategies, and classroom management, as well as student assessment, achievement, and learning styles into school counseling courses and experiential learning. Strengthening preservice school counselor knowledge and skills in these instruction-related areas can aid in abolishing teaching requirements for school counselor licensure, discussed in chapter 3, which continues on life support in a few states.

Bridging Contemporary Theory and Practice

Bridging theory and practice requires an understanding of current theoretical perspectives and a knowledge of past and current professional practices, as well as an understanding of the profession's future direction. Counselor educators stay abreast of current school reform legislation and trends in education in a number of ways. Visiting and shadowing local school counselors each academic year gives counselor educators a chance to partner with school counselors on research projects and co-present with counselors at conferences. Such interactions also provide counselor educators with information related to current practices and the realities of practice on a routine basis.

Reviewing recent research and literature that describes the strengths and shortcomings of school counseling practices and programming is an excellent way to strengthen counselor-educator programs and introduce preservice school counselors to the new roles and functions of the contemporary school counselor. An understanding of how the profession has developed and the obstacles we have overcome will promote a forward momentum for the new counseling paradigm.

Also essential are discussions about the importance of securing school administrator support for implementing a comprehensive school counseling program. Counselor educators are encouraged to invite school administrators from both the elementary and secondary levels to the classroom to speak candidly to school counselors in training, especially early in the coursework. It's also good practice to invite currently practicing school counselors into the classroom for roundtable discussions. Doses of reality early in the program aid in establishing an understanding of professional practice in a dynamic climate defined by accelerated change and school administrators (Mayes, Dollarhide, & Young, 2018).

Engaging preservice school counselors in experiential learning activities, particularly early in the program, enhances knowledge of school environments, norms, policies, and procedures and increases the ability to better bridge theory and practice. As preservice school counselors begin to develop an understanding of the relationship between theory and practice, practical approaches and tools are helpful for application. Teaching students to use cross-walking and alignment approaches such as standards blending meets CACREP standards, the recommendations of ASCA, and school improvement initiatives.

Introducing preservice school counselors to the countless forms and reporting tools used on a daily basis in the profession and provided in this text, such as the School Counseling Operational Plan for Effectiveness (SCOPE) and the School Counseling Operational Report of Effectiveness (SCORE) to document action plans, lesson plans, and results reports, will also aid students in understanding the steps involved in accountable programming (see chapter 6). These tools will also help school counselors to engage in accountable practices. Figure 5.1 shows a blank SCORE form; a sample SCORE form is shown in figure 5.2, and associated graphs are displayed in figure 5.3.

School counseling interns who share cross-walking strategies, data reporting tools, and ethically and legally sound forms during internships not only demonstrate accountability but also promote a reciprocal relationship.

SCORE
School Counseling Operational Report of Effectiveness

School   **Counselor**   **Date**

Activity Title

Goal(s)-Objective(s)

Data Collection and Evaluation

Number of Program Participants: Grade(s):   Other:

Type of Evaluation: ☐ Outcome   ☐ Process   ☐ Proximal   ☐ Distal

Data Source(s):

Details:

Method(s) of Data Analysis

☐ Percentages   ☐ Means/Averages   ☐ Frequencies   ☐ Counts   ☐ Statistical Testing   ☐
Other

Details:

Evaluation Outcome/ Program Impact

The program was Select One in meeting program goal(s) and targeted objectives(s) in the following area(s):

☐ Academic   ☐ Personal/Social   ☐ Career   ☐ Closing the Achievement Gap

Details:

Directions for Future Programming

☐ Continue Implementation of Current Activity   ☐ Modify Activity Based on Results

Details:

Pre-Post Data
Worksheet

Figure 5.1.   School Counseling Operational Report of Effectiveness (SCORE) report, blank

SCORE
School Counseling Operational Report of Effectiveness

School Virginia Public Schools   **Counselor** Schellenberg   **Date** 03/31/07

Activity Title

Resolving Conflict Peacefully and Enhancing Academic Achievment in Mathematics and Language Arts

Goal(s)-Objective(s)

To enhance students' personal/social, career, and academic development.

Objective 1: Students will define conflict, understand the nature of conflict, and be introduced to a positive approach to problem-solving for improving interpersonal relations.
Objective 2: Students will learn a 4-step problem-solving method.
Objective 3: Students will gain a better understanding of sets and fractional representations.

Data Collection and Evaluation

Number of Program Participants: 103   Grade(s): 2   Other:

Type of Evaluation: ☒ Outcome   ☐ Process   ☒ Proximal   ☐ Distal

Data Source(s): Pre-Post Lesson Assessment

Details: Classroom guidance activities were selected by grade level need. Assessment instrument developed from curriculum content to measure success in meeting objectives 1 and 3.

Method(s) of Data Analysis

☒ Percentages   ☒ Means/Averages   ☐ Frequencies   ☐ Counts   ☒ Statistical Testing   ☐ Other

Details: Student knowledge on the target topics was assessment immediately prior to the lesson and following the lesson using the same instrument.

Evaluation Outcome/Program Impact

The program was effective in meeting program goal(s) and targeted objectives(s) in the following area(s):

☒ Academic   ☒ Personal/Social   ☐ Career   ☐ Closing the Achievement Gap

Details: The standards blending lesson was effective in meeting both target objectives 1 and 3. Knowledge development occurred on both the school counseling and academic curriculum contents for students in all classrooms and for both subgroups, which was statistically significant as determined by paired sample t-tests. Independent sample t-tests indicated no significant differences between minority and non-minority proficiency levels on the core academic curriculum content. This would indicate the absence of an achievement gap between the two subgroups at pre- and post-lesson. Refer to the attached graphs.

Directions for Future Programming

☒ Continue Implementation of Current Activity ☐ Modify Activity Based on Results

Details: This program illustrates the significant impact of standards blending for teaching school counseling curriculum and reinforcing academic curriculum. Although, students had already been taught the mathematical concepts presented, there was a significant increase in proficiency as a result of the standards blending lesson.

Figure 5.2. School Counseling Operational Report of Effectiveness (SCORE) report, filled-out example

Interns have the potential to permeate settings where the traditionalist mind-set is dominant and cross-walking approaches and data reporting systems are absent or inadequate. These preservice school counselors, armed with contemporary tools and approaches, breathe life into dying practices.

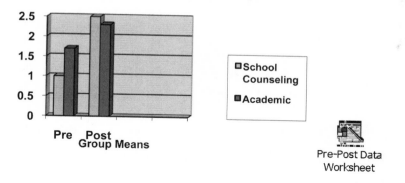

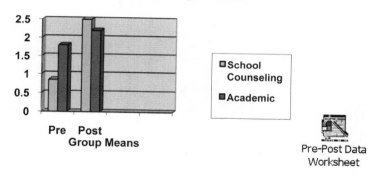

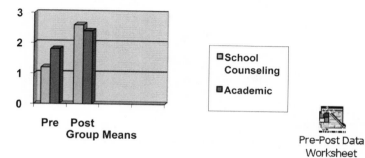

Figure 5.3. Associated SCORE graphs for figure 5.2.

Most importantly, counselor educators prepare future school counselors to be both counselors and educators, but first and foremost counselors. Counselor educators ensure that school counselors understand that their ultimate responsibility is to their client and that they must be knowledgeable of the law and apply professional ethics. Above all, they do no harm (Kitchener, 1984).

Research Collaboration

Collaborative research partnerships between counselor educators and school counseling practitioners are powerful partnerships with the potential to improve educational and professional school counseling practices and student academic achievement. It is vital to the continued growth of our profession that counselor educators take advantage of every opportunity to actively engage in collaborative research that adds to the body of literature and supports contemporary academic- and systems-focused school counseling programming.

Research collaboration with practitioners also addresses the immediate need to train currently practicing school counselors in data collection, data analysis, results interpretation, and program evaluation methodology, namely action research (Mason et al., 2016; Rosheim, 2018). School counselors who learn these essential skills through the research collaboration process are in a better position to continue engaging in evaluative studies that support the efficacy of contemporary programming. In turn, school counselors can provide counselor educators with access to the practice and research setting and an understanding of the unique and ever-changing needs of the school and division.

Collaborating on the publication of research outcomes aids in developing practitioner skills in scholarly publication while also promoting the positive impact and value of school counseling services on academic achievement and total student development. Publication informs and benefits all stakeholders, demonstrating how theory drives practice and how practice, in turn, informs theory.

SCHOOL COUNSELORS

If I had to summarize in one word what it takes to be a contemporary school counselor, it would be leadership. You cannot open recently published school counseling–focused books or journal articles without reading about the importance of leadership to the practice of school counseling. Not only does ASCA offer a School Counseling Leadership Specialist certification, but it provides you with the opportunity to see if you have a leadership mindset by taking the survey available on its website "Do You Have a Leadership Mindset?"

The school counselor as leader embraces the mindsets and practices that serve the whole student and contribute to academic achievement by using research to inform practice and embracing leadership models and characteristics known to maximize the performance of others and improve relationships, for example, social-emotional leadership (Bowers, Lemberger-Truelove, & Brigman, 2017) and transformative leadership (Shields, Dollarhide, & Young, 2017). Several characteristics define school counselor leadership practices: advocacy, equity, social justice, resourcefulness, problem solving, interconnectedness, moral courage, interpersonal influence, data-savvy, systemic collaboration, growth mindset, exemplary program design, and clear communication (Brougham & Kashubeck-West, 2017; Mayes et al., 2018; Michel et al., 2017; Shields, 2016; Shields et al., 2017; Young, Dollarhide, & Baughman, 2016).

Contemporary school counselors are committed to equitable, systemic change, often taking the data-driven road less traveled and applying approaches that directly and overtly align with academic development, including lesson plans, action plans, and results reports. Contemporary school counselors make use of technology to fortify accountability and professional advocacy, using an array of technologies to demonstrate the positive outcomes of school counseling programs on student learning and well-being.

Change, such as engaging in unfamiliar practices, can create internal struggle for many individuals, so resistance should be anticipated for contemporary-minded school counselors who may be entering into a traditionalist-minded school setting. In such cases, it's important to stay positive and focused—struggle strengthens you and creates growth. Although growth can be painful, you might emerge with a higher level of excellence, enthusiasm, and passion for the profession.

It is an exciting time to be a part of the school counseling profession as it continues to help establish the school counselor as an indispensable leader on the educational team. United in their efforts, a new age of progress and unprecedented maturity for the school counseling profession is imminent.

Contemporary Programming

Contemporary school counselors accept the challenge to implement systemic change, meet the holistic needs of students, and raise academic achievement for all students by:

- Gaining leadership and support of school administrators
- Establishing advisory committees
- Assuming the roles of both counselor and educator
- Programming that is both data-driven and data-producing
- Blending academic standards with the ASCA Mindsets and Behaviors for Student Success
- Developing research-supported curriculum
- Conducting program evaluations
- Using available technology
- Addressing the spiritual and religious needs of students
- Creating and disseminating action plans and results reports
- Collaborating and consulting with others
- Advocating for students, families, and the profession

Hashtag Technology

The digital age has broadened the school counselor's potential for the delivery of services at a higher quality and greater quantity. From Google docs and Prezi to Twitter and Facebook, billions of people use some type of digital device or app for professional and personal reasons, yet there are still school counselors who steer away from technology to the detriment of professional practices and more efficient—potentially even more effective—delivery of services (Gallo et al., 2015; Van Horn & Myrick, 2001). Research tells us that school counselors who embrace change and have positive mindsets regarding technology have been identified as the most successful (Anni, Sunawan & Haryono, 2018; Gallo et al., 2015). In turn, the use of technology has been linked to a better quality of education, improved academic performance, and positive classroom environments (Pierce & Cleary, 2016; Tarbutton, 2018).

It is important to gain an understanding of the latest and most popular digital devices and apps available so that you can educate your students on the risks of using the different technologies and provide information for using the devices and apps responsibly and safely. In fact, it is useful to offer workshops on this topic to teachers and parents. Counselors must practice good boundaries when interacting with students and parents digitally (Steele, Jacokes, & Stone, 2015). ASCA provides guidance by way of position statements on their website, one of which is called "The School Counselor and Student Safety and the Use of Technology" (ASCA, 2017). ASCA thoroughly covers the rationale for its position and what its believes to be the role of the school counselor in ensuring that students receive opportunities to become proficient in the use of technology and in the protection of their digital footprints.

Departmental websites and blogs are useful, broad reaching, and practical mediums for communication with stakeholders. These sites have the power to shape perceptions and effect change in systems that have not adopted contemporary school counseling practices. School counseling programs become that much more meaningful and credible when stakeholders understand their practices and programming and view the school counselor as a knowledgeable professional. In many cases, however, this information is still not being conveyed (Shimoni & Greenberger, 2015). School counseling websites should communicate information that aids students, teachers, and families, and advocates for the profession, such as: (1) school counselor roles and functions; (2) school counselor education, training, and credentials; (3) information regarding professional associations; (4) current trends and developments in the profession to include the ASCA model and the changed language; (5) mission statements and program goals that clearly connect school counseling to the academic achievement mission of schools; (6) resource links for students, teachers, and families; (7) nondiscrimination statements; (8) financial aid and scholarship information; and (9) programming and outcomes (Kennedy & Stanley, 2015; Shimoni & Greenberger, 2015).

Professional Identity and Advocacy

Promoting a unified professional identity and engaging in professional advocacy requires staying abreast of the research and current trends and developments that impact school counseling practices. Remaining proficient in the profession involves reading professional journals and newsletters, maintaining professional association memberships, attending conferences, and networking with counseling professionals within and outside of the school setting to include counselor educators. School counselors use this information to enhance practices and to promote unified roles, functions, and the changed language of the profession.

Lifelong learning is essential in this fledgling profession that is experiencing unprecedented change and rapid growth. Continuous professional development allows school counselors to astutely communicate with stakeholders about their dual roles and functions and to effectively meet the needs of students with the continuous improvement of practices, but let us not forget the familiar cliché—actions speak louder than words. Modeling the changed language of our profession and consistently demonstrating how school counseling programs contribute to academic achievement and total student development are thus the most effective means of professional advocacy and establishing a professional identity for school counselors. It's worth repeating: getting this information out to the general public by way of a school counseling webpage and blog is critical.

Teaming with other educators in the planning and delivery of services is another valuable way to advocate for the renewed profession that views collaboration as an endless resource, and the school counselor should actively seek out opportunities to work with colleagues, teachers, counselor educators, administrators, and parents. Standards blending provides an ideal opportunity for collaboration with classroom teachers, who genuinely appreciate the reinforcement of academic standards within and outside of the classroom. School counselors can team with resource teachers such as art and music teachers to provide creative and dramatic musicals and assemblies that involve students, include academic and school counseling standards, and can be presented to the entire student body. This is also a great way to get parents and the community involved in programming.

They can also make a difference outside the school that will positively affect practices inside of the school. School counselors might consider attending and presenting at professional education and counseling conferences and in the community, joining or establishing a regional school counseling leadership team, joining professional associations, serving as an officer on professional associations or credentialing boards, and engaging in research collaboration with counselor educators.

Finally, school counselors might also consider lecturing about contemporary and academic-focused school counseling topics at staff development meetings to an audience of school administrators and teachers. School administrators appreciate insight into the changes that are occurring in the school counseling profession and value fresh ideas as to how those changes can enhance student achievement and contribute to school improvement.

School counselors know how school counseling makes a difference in the lives of children, but we have been negligent in demonstrating an overt alignment with, and direct impact on, academic achievement. We have also been lax in providing stakeholders with essential documentation that demonstrates accountable practices and positive program outcomes that establish the value of our profession. It is time to get off the sidelines and into the game—the clock is ticking, and many are keeping score!

SCHOOL COUNSELOR SUPERVISORS

School counselor supervisors are in a unique position to represent the interests of both school administrators and school counselors. The traditional paradigm was somewhat problematic for the school counselor supervisor, who had some difficulty defining how the school counselor's roles and functions clearly contributed to academic achievement and aligned with the school's mission. The implied nature of their contributions to student development, primarily academic achievement, has not been enough to fully secure support for school counseling programs.

The compatible interests and aligned missions of school administrators and contemporary school counselors, however, now provide enthusiastic school counselor supervisors with a new platform from which to promote change, professional identity, and a unified profession, as well as advocate on behalf of school counselors.

Still, many school counselor supervisors have not received sufficient training in clinical supervision (Brown et al., 2018; Merlin & Brendel, 2017). This is an area that remains a concern for school counselors, who need more than administrative supervision. School counselors who serve as on-site supervisors for interns in graduate school as a way to meet licensure requirements have the benefit of receiving supervision by the university desiring to place the student. Some schools offer these training sessions locally or online. School counselor supervisors who do not have this training are encouraged to seek out such opportunities by way of conference workshops, graduate course work, or through a local university that offers these opportunities, as noted above, for potential site supervisors.

School counselor supervisors should also aid in the recruitment and selection of highly qualified school counselors, which calls for an understanding of what constitutes a highly qualified school counselor. Counselor supervisors ensure the continued preparation of school counselors by supporting and encouraging continuous professional development and advanced level credentialing.

Implementing School Counselor Roles and Functions

School counselor supervisors must create school counselor job descriptions and performance evaluations to reflect the new vision school counselor's roles and functions at the elementary and secondary levels, and they can refer to the CACREP standards, ASCA national model, TSCI, state standards for school counseling programs, and this text for guidance in redefining school counselor duties and responsibilities. Job descriptions and performance expectations identify the essential functions of school counselors at each educational level. This is particularly important for pertinent school counselor performance evaluation and for identifying job-related search criteria for school counselor recruitment and selection.

Selecting Contemporary School Counselors

Principals do not generally have a background or education in school counseling and may be unaware of the contemporary roles and functions of school counselors, yet they are often responsible for hiring school counselors. Therefore, it is imperative that school counselor supervisors provide guidance to school administrators in selecting well-prepared school counselors who understand and support the new direction of the profession.

The level of guidance provided by the school counselor supervisor is largely dependent on the size of the school and school district. Guidance may entail working closely with principals to provide selection criteria and standardized interview questions. Guidance might also require the supervisor's direct participation in the screening of applications and interviewing of prospective school counselor candidates.

Professional Development

This book provides school counselor supervisors with the information, approaches, and tools for fulfilling their administrative supervision role. These supervisors, however, particularly those with little or no formal supervision training, are urged to continue their education and professional development specific to counselor supervision as noted earlier in this chapter. Understanding and developing the ability to apply models of counselor supervision is vital to the optimal functioning of the individual school counselor as well as the school counseling team.

In addition to their education and progressive credentials, school counselor supervisors add to their credibility as effective leaders by remaining actively involved in the profession. School counselor supervisors are expected to maintain professional association membership, present at conferences, publish in peer-reviewed journals, and collaborate with counselor educators.

When school counselors view counselor supervisors as credible, they are more likely to be open to their leadership and to actively seek out their supervisors for opportunities to develop higher-level knowledge and skills. In addition to credibility, school counselor supervisors must be viewed as approachable, nonconfrontational, and nonjudgmental. An atmosphere that welcomes questions, views mistakes as an opportunity for growth, and demonstrates a team approach to obtaining answers is conducive to learning and optimal functioning. In the absence of approachable school counselor supervisors, school counselors may seek answers from colleagues, which may or may not be the correct way to get answers to their questions.

It is important for school counselor supervisors to accept that they cannot and will not know it all. While an approachable attitude and advanced education and counselor credentials are essential to optimal administrative and clinical competence, as well as effective leadership, having all the answers is not. Our ever-changing, global workforce is exceedingly specialized. An effective leader is a resourceful visionary who consults with those most knowledgeable in a specific area or program and engages in a needs-driven, team approach to decision making, process and program implementation, and systemic change.

Changing traditional ways of responding to student needs is particularly challenging for even the most adept school counselors. The reform-minded supervisor is a lifeline for school counselors who are not knowledgeable about, or are having difficulty implementing, contemporary and academic-focused practices. Supervisors provide school counselors with information, resources, tools, and approaches for implementing accountable, comprehensive school counseling programs that align with district and state academic achievement missions.

Encouraging the use of standards blending as part of a comprehensive school counseling program clearly aligns the program with the academic achievement mission of schools. Including SCOPE and SCORE as tools to be used by school counselors for developing accountable programs and documenting impact data provides counselor supervisors with advocacy instruments to share with school administrators.

School counselor supervisors should model desired practices and provide professional development opportunities to school counselors for understanding and fulfilling their dual roles and functions. As newly acquired knowledge and skills are applied and the school counseling program begins to transform, so, too, does the individual school counselor, which may create unanticipated conflict and discomfort for some. It is important for school counseling supervisors to understand, therefore, that in the midst of change, even the most seasoned school counselors may experience many of the same thoughts and feelings of uncertainty and dependency of a beginning school counselor. School counselor supervisors should anticipate the struggle, foresee the stumbling, and meet it with encouragement, problem solving, and a focus on what is being learned while on the road to discovery. This is an instance where understanding developmental models of counselor supervision is extremely useful. It may be necessary to temporarily adjust levels of counselor supervision until the challenged school counselor regains his or her self-perception of competence and stability.

Meeting challenges with a positive attitude and a focus on a shared vision for school counseling may aid in reducing resistance while individuals and the system seek to reestablish homeostasis. Although the road may seem long, the outcome is worth the journey.

SCHOOL ADMINISTRATORS

It has been two decades since implementation of a new vision for school counseling began, but there is still a dearth of commentary in the field on this major development, with many school counseling programs continuing to go about business as usual. Several factors are contributing to this reluctance or inability to cede the traditional school counseling paradigm.

Some within the profession fear that the new paradigm threatens the status quo and so remain shackled to traditional mental health– and individual-focused practices. Others simply prefer the comfort of complacency over change, or they recognize the need for change but feel a lack of support, practical processes, approaches, and tools for implementing change.

School administrators have not been fully informed, or have been misinformed, regarding this new paradigm, but school administrator leadership is the essential missing link to institutionalizing a comprehensive school counseling program that fully attends to the holistic needs of students. Since the success of the school counseling program is inextricably tied to school administrator acceptance and stewardship, therefore, this text is designed to (1) serve as the communication conduit for understanding contemporary school counseling mindsets and practices and the inherent dual roles and functions of the school counselor, (2) provide the impetus for the development of a symbiotic relationship between school administrators and school counselors, (3) promote the implementation of comprehensive school counseling programs that promote the holistic development of students and focus on universal academic achievement, and (4) emphasize the importance of school counselor and school counselor supervisor selection and promotion practices in ensuring highly qualified school counseling teams driven by a shared vision.

SUPPORTING CONTEMPORARY SCHOOL COUNSELING PRACTICES AND A UNIFIED PROFESSIONAL IDENTITY

Over the years, school counselors have been assigned duties and responsibilities that are unrelated to school counseling due to inconsistent pedagogies in counselor education, role ambiguity, and a lack of accountability in professional practices. For example, many school counselors are charged with maintaining student records; supervising study halls; serving as meeting secretaries; acting as teachers, substitute teachers, and disciplinarians; operating attendance tables; and assisting the front office clerical staff. Studies show that assignment to noncounseling duties are taking up to 50 percent of school counselors' time (Burnham & Jackson, 2000) and are not cost efficient or an effective use of manpower (Hardesty & Dillard, 1994).

School counselors could instead be identifying low-achieving populations and developing programs designed to have a direct positive impact on achievement gaps. School counselors could also be applying systems-focused strategies to enhance student motivation to learn and graduate from school. The school counselor's time would also be better spent collaborating with teachers to implement standards blending in classrooms and small groups.

While ushering in an exciting new age of contemporary school counseling practices, school administrators can expect to encounter resistance akin to challenging the big bang theory. Resistance is a hurdle to overcome and one that is not new to school administrators. School counselors and school counselor supervisors with an allegiance to the traditional mindsets are likely to challenge those who are diving into contemporary practices. Such challenges are lamentable but not unanticipated and must be met with analytic simplicity—academic-focused practices are recognized in the profession as essential, pragmatic, and theoretically sound and in the best interest of all stakeholders.

Selecting Contemporary School Counselor Supervisors

School administrators are vicariously responsible for the actions and inactions of school counseling practitioners. As such, it is in the best interest of school administrators to look beyond the minimal competencies of master's degrees and mandatory licensure by states when selecting school counselors and school counselor supervisors. As more school administrators base their selection and promotion decisions on a preference for school counselors who hold advanced-level credentialing, more school counseling practitioners will seek to obtain such credentials. ASCA offers information regarding the purpose, duties, responsibilities, and required and desired qualifications of a school counselor supervisor on its website listed in chapter 1. The need for at least one highly qualified school counselor supervisor in each school division who is qualified to provide both clinical and administrative supervision has been well documented.

Well-qualified school counselor supervisor candidates should have a track record of presentation, publication, and self-initiated professional development demonstrative of a passion for the profession. Active participation in the profession leads to a deeper knowledge and understanding of contemporary school counseling practices and is clearly demonstrated by the use of the contemporary language of the profession (e.g., school counselor versus guidance counselor). Highly qualified school counselor supervisors have the education, training, and credentials to provide both clinical and administrative supervision. Potential school counselor supervisors, for example, should hold the credentials of National Certified Counselor (NCC), National Certified School Counselor (NCSC), and Licensed Professional Counselor (LPC), which are indicative of optimal preparation as a school counselor.

Advanced voluntary credentials also demonstrate a commitment to professional development and a motivation toward professional advancement and skills improvement. Ideally, school counselor supervisors will possess a doctoral degree in counselor education and supervision from a CACREP-accredited, program.

Having administrative and clinical expertise is also essential to school counselor leadership, and those who have had such supervision experience will demonstrate enhanced counseling skills, effectiveness, and accountability; increased confidence and competence; and more motivation for professional development (Agnew, Vaught, Getz, & Fortune, 2000; Brown et al., 2018; Crutchfield & Borders, 1997; Merlin & Brendel, 2017).

Clinical supervision also assists school counselors in enhancing their own counseling and decision-making skills for more effective management of complex cases and for ensuring optimal student development and a safe school environment. Responding adequately to student needs that may involve severe depression, homicide and suicide ideation, substance abuse, school violence, child abuse, and pregnancy, for example, requires that school counseling practitioners apply proficient clinical skills and knowledge of the legal and ethical implications of their actions or inactions. For these reasons, school counselors have expressed their desire and need for meaningful administrative and clinical supervision in order to remain competent, but studies have found that most school counselors are not receiving clinical supervision of any kind due to a lack of highly qualified school counselor supervisors or clinical supervision training (Brown et al., 2018; Merlin & Brendel, 2017; Kaffenberger, Murphy, & Bemak, 2006; Page, Pietrzak, & Sutton, 2001).

Limited qualified applicant pools have resulted in the promotion of practicing school counselors as a result of their performance as school counselors, or the promotion of individuals with higher education or supervisory experience in areas other than school counseling. Proficiency as a school counselor or an administrator trained in other educational fields, however, does not equal a proficient school counselor supervisor.

Although such practices may have been necessary in some cases, research has revealed that school counselor supervisors who lack specialized education in counselor supervision tend to shy away from the clinical aspects of enhancing counseling knowledge and skills, thereby providing insufficient clinical supervision (Brown et al., 2018; Merlin & Brendel, 2017). Insufficient clinical supervision, which includes the ethical and legal implications of counseling minors in the schools, leaves many school districts chronically vulnerable to litigation.

School counselors and others who aspire to provide administrative and clinical counselor supervision should therefore seek to acquire advanced education and credentialing in preparation for such a role. It is not recommended that time spent in the role of school counselor be considered sufficient for promotion to counselor supervisor or director—it is not a rite of passage. School counselors who have a passion for the profession, a desire to bring about change, and an aspiration to become highly competent, effective leaders will seek to enhance their educational credentials above the minimum criteria and contribute to the profession through additional research, service, presentation, and publication. These are the school counselors who have truly prepared for the clinical and administrative roles of counselor supervisor.

As noted earlier, school administrators can encourage advanced-level education and credentialing for school counselors by demonstrating this preference in their promotion and selection decisions and offering stipends for advanced voluntary credentials—by both NBPTS and NBCC. Additionally, pay supplements or higher salaries for school counselor directors and supervisors are a financial investment that will prove to have substantial returns for all stakeholders.

SUMMARY

Decades of political winds have shifted the educational climate shaping our nation's schools. School counselors have traditionally been left out of educational reform agendas, viewed as noncontributors, and burdened with large student caseloads because they could not provide evidence of how they made a difference in the lives of students and how our programming has positively impacted academic achievement—the primary mission of schools.

Concern for the future of the profession and recognition of the need to align school counseling programs with academic achievement, however, has prompted an unparalleled change in school counseling. Contemporary practices require a continuing shift in counselors' mindsets in both the preparation and practice of counseling. It is an exciting and challenging time to be a part of the school counseling profession, with much work to be done and significant changes to be made—together.

Chapter Six

Tools of the Trade

The call for accountability in school counseling practices is not new, and it has heightened efforts to prepare, encourage, and support school counselor efforts toward accountable practices (Sink, 2018). Throughout this text, I have discussed data-driven practices, standards-based program planning, research-supported curriculum and counseling approaches, and program evaluation as a means of improving practices and demonstrating accountability. To further clarify the construct of accountability, the following statement is offered: "To be accountable means being responsible for one's actions and contributions, especially in terms of objectives, procedures, and results" (Myrick, 2003, p. 175).

MATERIALS MOST FREQUENTLY USED BY SCHOOL COUNSELORS

The materials used by school counselors as a part of daily practices and processes aid in demonstrating accountability, credibility, cultural sensitivity, and ethically and legally sound practices. This chapter identifies the daily materials most frequently used by school counselors. Since these materials, created using Microsoft Word, are not always provided or up-to-date in the preparation or practice setting, the website downloads include the following materials for the purposes noted.

- Action plan template: School Counseling Operational Plan for Effectiveness (SCOPE)

- Case notes: Essential note-keeping elements
- Child abuse report: Suspected child abuse reporting
- Core school counseling curriculum communication to teachers (beginning of year)
- Informed consent: Parental consent for small-group and individual counseling services
- Informed consent: Parental consent for sensitive classroom lessons/assemblies
- Opt-out-of-school counseling form
- Referral for school counseling services by teacher or administrator
- Referral for school counseling services by parent
- Referral for school counseling services: Elementary student self-referral
- Referral for school counseling services: Secondary student self-referral
- Release of school counseling case notes and sharing of information
- Results report template: School Counseling Operational Report of Effectiveness (SCORE)
- Suicide ideation report: Suspected suicide reporting

Action Plans and Lesson Plans

ASCA has underscored the importance of actions plans and lesson plans in documenting program and lesson activities and the result of those activities on student development and academic achievement. Abraham Lincoln declared, "Give me six hours to chop down a tree and I will spend the first four sharpening the axe." Lincoln's statement clearly depicts the time-consuming and important nature of planning.

Action plans and lesson plans are important to share with school administrators in particular because they can help gain the support of other stakeholders. Studies indicate that stakeholder support and partnerships enhance school climate and increase the likelihood of a student's success in school and in life (Bryan, 2005; Cooper, 2002). School counselors who involve stakeholders in program planning and routinely provide them with information about school counseling activities help establish positive alliances and maintain program momentum.

The School Counseling Operational Plan for Effectiveness (SCOPE) is a Microsoft Office template intended to streamline action planning and lesson planning. The SCOPE template (see figure 6.1) makes use of check boxes and text boxes to walk the user through the process of accountable program planning. SCOPE meets the programming requirements and essential components of the ASCA-recommended (2012, 2014) action plans, closing-the-achievement-gap action plans, and lesson plans, and is used in partnership with SCORE, the School Counseling Operational Report of Effectiveness, which is the second part of the two-part data reporting template. It demonstrates essential components of a comprehensive school counseling program that aligns with academic achievement missions and is discussed later in this chapter.

Case Notes

Counseling session case notes need to be maintained in a confidential manner (e.g., locked in a filing cabinet or secured in password-protected electronic files). There are differences in the confidentiality and reporting requirements of case notes that are sole possession notes and those that are formal

Figure 6.1

SCOPE
School Counseling Operational Plan for Effectiveness

School Counselor: Others:

Action Plan/Lesson Plan Date: Title:

☐ Small Group   ☐ School Counseling Curriculum   ☐ Individual Student Planning

Need/Purpose:

☐ Closing the Gap Strategy   Data Used to Identify Gap Population:

Target Population: Students in Grade(s):   Projected Number of Participants:
          Other:

Goal:

Objective(s):

Core Subjects & Academic Standards Addressed:
☐ Mathematics
☐ Language Arts
☐ Science
☐ Social Studies
☐ Other

School Counseling Standards: Mindsets and Behaviors:
☐ Academic
☐ Social-Emotional
☐ Career

Plan for Evaluation: ☐ Outcome   ☐ Process   ☐ Perception   ☐ Proximal   ☐ Distal
          Data Sources:

Curriculum (Number of Sessions/Lessons: Timeline:):

Figure 6.1.   Action plan template: School Counseling Operational Plan for Effectiveness (SCOPE)

case notes (Schellenberg, 2018). Formal case notes are objective in nature, while sole possession case notes are often more subjective.

Although school counseling case notes now fall under the Family Educational Rights and Privacy Act (FERPA), school counselors are well advised to consider the Health Insurance Portability and Accountability Act (HIPAA) when creating formal case notes because of the advanced level of credentials many school counselors are beginning to earn that supplement department of education school counselor licensure (Schellenberg, 2018). These credentials may, at some point in time, be viewed as equivalent to mental health care providers and thus fall under the watchful eye of HIPAA, which requires specific objective formal case note information, noted below and included on the Case Notes form on the website (see figure 6.2):

- Dates of sessions
- Number of sessions
- Assessment data
- Presenting problem
- Treatment and counseling plan
- Information related to collaboration and consultation with others
- Session notes
- Associated documents (e.g., informed consent, drawings, letters, referrals)

Child Abuse Reporting

There are multiple types—and many possible signs—of both child abuse and child neglect of which school counselors need to be aware (Schellenberg, 2018). School counselors are mandated to report suspected child abuse and neglect. Information on violence prevention and child abuse and neglect and the mandated reporting requirements, along with Child Abuse and Neglect Training Modules, are available at www.childwelfare.gov/preventing/developing/training.cfm.

School counselors are also required to report suspected child abuse and neglect within a specific time period, which is generally anywhere from twenty-four to seventy-two hours. School counselors need to know the specific requirements of the law in their state. The Child Abuse Report on the website walks school counselors through reporting requirements (see figure 6.3).

School Name (HERE)

School Counseling Case Notes

Counselor Name: _____   Date of session: _____

Student Name: _____   Session # _____ of _____

Presenting issue(s):

Assessment/Appraisal data:

Counseling Plan:

Collaboration/Consultation Information (Who, When, How, Why, What)

Session Notes (objective):

(Attach any related documents such as drawings, letters, referrals, informed consent)

Figure 6.2.   Case notes (essential note-keeping elements)

Core School Counseling Curriculum Communication to Teachers

School counselors generally supply teachers with a communication and core
school counseling curriculum schedule at the beginning of each year. This
communication may be emailed, placed in teacher boxes, or posted on elec-

School Name HERE

Child Abuse/Neglect Reporting
(Know your state's reporting timeline, generally no more than 72 hours)

Student Name: _____   Grade: _____   Today's Date: _____

School Counselor Reporting: _____

Parent-Guardian: _____   Home Phone: _____   Work/Cell: _____

Who is suspected of the abuse/neglect? _____   Relationship to student: _____
    Address: _____   Phone: _____

Date suspected abuse occurred: _____   Time: _____   Place of suspected abuse: _____

Date suspected abuse reported to school counselor: _____   Time: _____

How was the suspected abuse disclosed: _____

Student's emotional state at the time of disclosure: _____

Names and ages of siblings: _____

Describe nature of suspected abuse (e.g., sexual, physical, emotional) or neglect (e.g., physical, educational), and identify specific body parts (scars, bruises, cuts, etc. do not have to be visible).
_____
_____
_____

Have the information above completed when contacting Child Protective Services/law enforcement.

Date of report by school counselor to CPS/law enforcement: _____   Time of report: _____

CPS/law enforcement Contact Name: _____

Information given to the CPS/law enforcement contact (based on information noted above):
_____
_____
_____

Time child or adolescent scheduled to leave school on date of report: _____

Let CPS/law enforcement know if child or adolescent needs to be seen immediately (e.g., child scared to go home, you are concerned for the child if they go home unaccompanied by CPS/law enforcement).

Actions taken by CPS/law enforcement:
_____
_____

Figure 6.3.   Child abuse report (suspected child abuse reporting)

tronic bulletin boards and intranet systems. The communication briefly introduces the school counselor's services and the process for services delivery. The document includes the schedule for delivery of core school counseling curriculum with an invitation to teachers to identify additional topics they would like the school counselor to address. The communication also offers teachers the opportunity to change the day or time of scheduled school counseling curriculum delivery to something more convenient to their class schedule and planned activities. A general form is provided on the website and may vary significantly, depending upon what the school counselor would like to relay to teachers at the start of each school year (see figure 6.4).

Informed Consent

Two informed consent forms are included on the ancillary website, https://textbooks.rowman.com/schellenberg. One is for Parental Consent for Sensitive Classroom Lessons/Assemblies (see figure 6.5). The other form is for Parental Consent for Small Group/Individual Counseling Services (see figure 6.6).

Parental Consent for Sensitive Classroom Lessons and Assemblies should be obtained when the topic to be covered is sensitive or graphic in nature. For example, if a school counselor is implementing core school counseling curriculum entitled "Internet Safety," and the content includes topics like abduction, sexual assault, homicide, etc., then the school counselor will want to

Name of School HERE

Classroom Guidance Curriculum Communication to Teachers (Beginning of the Year)

Hello Teachers!

As you plan for a great year, I wanted to provide you with information about the services I offer to support you and your students. I offer small groups and individual counseling aimed at addressing the immediate needs of your students. The *Referral for School Counseling Services by Teacher/Administrator* is available in my office. Parents, too, may refer their child/adolescent for school counseling services. Please refer interested parents to me. I will be communicating my services to parents during our first PTA/PTSA meeting. Students may use the *Self-Referral* forms located in the box outside my office door, as needed. I will explain this procedure to students during the beginning of the year assembly.

[Secondary school counselors will also want to say, "I also offer individual student planning aimed at readying students for life after high school" and describe the process for reaching every student in your school.]

The classroom guidance schedule for each of your classes is listed below. Please let me know immediately if the date and time I have selected to deliver the guidance curriculum is not convenient and we will work together to select a day and time that is best for you. The topics are selected based on a review of school data and/or based on the delivery of a comprehensive school counseling program that attends to the developmental needs of students and addresses specific school counseling student standards and competencies. If you would like me to conduct additional guidance lessons for your class, please provide me with the topic you would like me to cover and we'll schedule a date and time for curriculum delivery.

Please do not hesitate to contact me if you have concerns about one or more of your students. I am here to support you in any way I can.

[Classroom Guidance Schedule Here]

Kindest regards,

Signature Here
Email Here

Figure 6.4.   Core school counseling curriculum communication to teachers (beginning of year)

School Name (HERE)

Sensitive Topic Classroom Guidance/Assembly Informed Consent

Dear Parent or Guardian,

This is to inform you that the school counselor(s) at your student's school is coordinating/conducting a classroom guidance lesson/assembly that involves information of a sensitive nature.

The topic to be covered is _____ and will be presented by _____. The following are more details regarding the content of the program to be delivered:

(Insert curriculum to be covered in the activities/program HERE)

_____

Consent:

I, _____, have read and understand the contents of this informed consent.
    (please print name)

I give my child permission to participate in the proposed counseling activities/program.

Parent/Guardian Signature:_____ Date:_____

Figure 6.5.   Informed consent (parental consent for sensitive classroom lessons/assemblies)

seek parental consent. Otherwise, school counselors do not generally seek parental consent for the delivery of core school counseling curriculum intended to be educational in nature and afforded to all students. When in doubt, err on the side of caution and provide parents with an opportunity to opt their student out of such activities by providing them with the topic, description, and the date and time of the activity.

School counselors are not legally obligated to obtain parental permission prior to group or individual counseling unless there is a federal or state statute to the contrary (Remley & Herlihy, 2014; Stone, 2009). As a matter of best practices, however, many school division policies require that school counselors obtain parental consent, particularly if counseling will extend beyond one or two sessions (Stone, 2009). For this reason, the second informed consent form in this text is for Parental Consent for Small Group/ Individual Counseling Services.

School Name HERE
Parent/Guardian Consent for Individual and Group School Counseling Services

This is to inform you that your student, _____, has been referred to the school counselor by
_____ for concerns related to:

☐ Academic   ☐Behavior   ☐Interpersonal ☐ Personal   ☐ Career

School Counselor will conduct counseling services via:
☐Individual counseling ☐Individual student planning   ☐ Small group counseling

Topics to be covered during the counseling sessions may include one or more of the following:

☐Emotional Concerns   ☐Academic Performance   ☐ Career
☐Behavioral Concerns   ☐Interpersonal Relationships

Additional information: _____
_____

School counseling sessions are generally 20-30 minutes. Counseling sessions will take place in the school in an environment that supports the confidential nature of counselor-student relationship.
Confidentiality: Information revealed between the school counselor and student during the counseling session is confidential. It is the ethical responsibility of the counselor to safeguard students from unauthorized disclosures of information shared in the context of the counseling sessions. The school counselor seeks to establish alliances with parents and educators that are in the best interest of the student. Limitations to confidentiality include:

✓ When student poses danger to self, others, or the property of others.
✓ When counselor suspects abuse/neglect.
✓ Upon authorization of parent/student.
✓ Under court order.

In some circumstances school counselors may be required to breach confidentiality as a matter of school policy. These limitations will be discussed with students during initial counseling sessions. The importance of confidentiality is stressed during group sessions, but cannot be guaranteed between group members.

Consent:

I, _____, have read and understand the contents of this informed consent.
   (please print name)

I give my student permission to participate in the proposed school counseling services.

Parent/Guardian Signature:_____ Date:_____

Figure 6.6.   Informed consent (parental consent for small group/individual counseling services)

Opt Out of School Counseling

School counselors are strongly encouraged to ensure that every parent receives an Opt Out of School Counseling form (see figure 6.7). Generally, this form is included in the student handbook. Parents who wishes to opt their children or adolescents out of individual counseling, individual student planning, or group counseling may complete and return the form to the school counselor. Even when parents opt their children out of counseling services, the school counselor may see the student if that meeting is deemed essential to maintaining immediate order in the school.

Referral for School Counseling Services

Four of the Referral for School Counseling Services forms are shown in figures 6.8 through 6.11 and are included on the ancillary website. One form is provided for each of the following populations: (1) teacher or administrator, (2) parent, (3) elementary self-referral, and (4) secondary self-referral. These forms are simple in nature to ease the referral process. The teacher/administrator form asks if the parent is aware of the issues or the referral to

Name of School HERE

Opt Out of School Counseling Services

Dear Parent or Guardian,

School counseling services are provided to your student as part of his or her educational services. If you **do not** wish to allow you student to participate in any of the services listed below please place a check mark by the service that you do not wish the school counselor to provide. Please keep in mind that even if you opt your child out of individual counseling services, a school counselor may have sessions with your child throughout the school year if doing so is warranted in order to maintain order in the school.

Individual student planning is not listed, since school counselors must meet with secondary level students for scheduling and academic/career planning. The school counselor's instructional curriculum delivered in the classroom is not listed since those services are a part of the school curriculum afforded to all students. If classroom instruction (or another program) by the school counselor is of a sensitive nature, you will be informed and allowed the opportunity to opt your student out of those specific programs. Thank you for the opportunity to work with your student!

Please do nothing if you want your child to participate in school counseling services as noted above.

Please place a check mark(s) by the school counseling service you wish to opt your student out of:

☐ Small Group Counseling   ☐ Individual Counseling

_____   _____
Name of Parent or Guardian (please print)   Name of Student (please print)

_____   _____
Parent/Guardian Signature   Date

Parent/Guardian Telephone Information:

Home: _____

Work: _____

Cell: _____

Figure 6.7.   Opt out of school counseling form

the school counselor. This is to promote good parent-teacher relations. Parents should be made aware of concerns that teachers or administrators have about their children or adolescents prior to referral to the school counselor, unless a teacher or administrator suspects child abuse.

Release of School Counseling Case Notes and Sharing of Information

Most schools have a release-of-records form, so school counselors should know the school's policy regarding that form. In the absence of a policy, a specific form, or if the school counselor is permitted to use his or her own

School Name HERE

Teacher and Administrator Referral for School Counseling Services

Referral Source: _____ Relationship to Student: _____

Student Name: _____ Grade: _____

Reason(s) for Referral: Academic _____ Behavior _____ Social _____ Emotional _____

Please describe circumstances/concern: _____

_____

What strategies have been taken to date to mediate concern: _____

_____

_____

How might the concern noted be impacting the student academically, emotionally, and/or socially:

_____

Please explain any external factors that you feel the counselor needs to know: _____

_____

_____

Has the parent been informed of your concerns? _____ Yes _____ No

If not, please explain: _____

Has the parent been informed of this referral to school counseling services? ___ Yes _____ No

If not, please explain: _____

Figure 6.8. Referral for school counseling services by teacher/administrator

School Name HERE

Parent Referral (consent included) for School Counseling Services

Student Name (please print full name): _____

Parent/Guardian Making Referral (please print): _____
    Relationship to Student: _____ (e.g., mother, father)

Reason(s) for Referral: Academic _____ Behavior _____ Social _____ Emotional _____

Please describe circumstances/concern: _____
_____

What strategies have been taken to date to mediate concern: _____
_____

How might the concern noted be impacting the student academically, emotionally, and/or socially:
_____

Please explain any external factors that you feel the school counselor needs to know: _____
_____
_____

Has the teacher been informed of your concerns? _____ Yes _____ No
If not, please explain: _____

Has the teacher been informed of this referral to school counseling services? ___ Yes _____ No
If not, please explain: _____

Confidentiality: Information revealed between the school counselor and student during the counseling session is confidential. It is the ethical responsibility of the counselor to safeguard students from unauthorized disclosures of information shared in the context of the counseling sessions. The school counselor seeks to establish alliances with parents and educators that are in the best interest of the student. Limitations to confidentiality include:

    ✓ When student poses danger to self, others, or the property of others.
    ✓ When counselor suspects abuse/neglect.
    ✓ Upon authorization of parent/student.
    ✓ Under court order.

In some circumstances school counselors may be required to breach confidentiality as a matter of school policy. These limitations will be discussed with students during initial counseling sessions. The importance of confidentiality is stressed during group sessions, but cannot be guaranteed between group members.

Informed Consent:

I give my student permission to participate school counseling services.

Parent/Guardian Signature:_____ Date:_____

Figure 6.9. Referral for school counseling services by parent

form, the Release of School Counseling Case Notes and Sharing of Information form is provided on the ancillary website (see figure 6.12). School counselors must obtain written permission from the parent and consent from the student prior to sharing student information.

    There are times when a school counselor is encouraged by the parent to share documents or communications with outside counselors (or others with a legitimate interest in the well-being of the student) to aid in helping the student. School counselors who are comfortable sharing the information obtained in the counselor-student relationship should get parental consent in writing and ensure student assent.

School Name HERE

I Want to See the School Counselor

My Name is: _____

My Teacher is: _____

I am in grade: _____

Today's date is: _____

If you want to see the school counselor today draw a circle around the mouse!

Figure 6.10. **Referral for school counseling services (elementary student self-referral)**

School Name HERE

Please complete this form to see the school counselor:

Date:_____

Your Name: _____

My School Counselor's Name: _____

Do you need to see the school counselor today: Circle one: YES   NO

Please list your teachers and times in each class:

Teachers	Class Times

Figure 6.11. **Referral for school counseling services (secondary student self-referral)**

Results Reports

Service logs have historically been used to document time spent on tasks and illustrate the numerous and diverse duties and levels of responsibilities of the school counselor. Although services delivered have their value in identifying what it is that school counselors do, they are inadequate in an outcome-driven educational environment. As the axiom goes, we are drowning in information but starved for knowledge. Documenting services delivered does not and should not replace program evaluation.

The knowledge we seek can be obtained by translating data into meaningful reports. Alas, this task can be time consuming and cumbersome, especially when exacerbated by daunting workloads. Nonetheless, creating documents that demonstrate activity outcomes enhances accountability. The School Counseling Operational Report of Effectiveness (SCORE) is a Microsoft Office template intended to streamline the results reporting process and meet the essential component guidelines for both results reporting and closing-the-achievement-gap results reporting recommended by ASCA (2012). SCORE is the second part of a two-part data reporting template specifically designed for school counseling programs. SCORE used in partnership with SCOPE demonstrates essential components of a comprehensive school counseling program that aligns with academic achievement missions, documenting both action plans (or lesson plans) and results reports.

SCORE (see figure 6.13) is designed to walk the user through the process of accountable program evaluation using form check boxes, text boxes, and drop-down menus. SCORE eases the process of data analysis, providing users with a preformulated Excel worksheet that contains protected formulas and accommodates up to five thousand data sets.

SCORE also allows for graphic illustrations as desired. Figure 6.14 illustrates what the user will see once the graph icon on the template is double-clicked. The user simply enters the pre- and postprogram data and lets the spreadsheet do the rest.

The worksheet can be used to calculate means and percentages of difference for up to five thousand data sets. Pre- and postprogram data are typed into columns A and B. The preprogram mean score appears in column C; the postprogram mean score appears in column D. The percentage of difference from pre- to postprogram measure appears in column E.

The SCORE worksheet can be used to analyze perception and outcome data for an entire school's population, individual students, a single class, multiple classes, grade levels, special populations, and specific question clusters for determining change and growth in targeted areas such as school counseling curriculum components, language arts components, and mathematics components. The worksheet can be copied for the inclusion of multiple worksheets in order to disaggregate data, or the worksheet can be deleted for exclusion from the report. The worksheet can also be saved (use the "save as" function) for storing data in a folder apart from the template.

School Name HERE
Release of School Counseling Case Notes and Sharing of Information

Signing of this document authorizes the school counselor, _____, to release counseling case notes and to share counseling related information with _____ for the following student:

_____ .

The school counselor and parent/guardian have discussed the purpose of these communications with the above named student and the student is in agreement with the sharing of information between the school counseling and the above named professional.

This release form does not authorize release of academic records and other documents housed in the student's academic record. Parents seeking the release of information contained in the student's academic record should contact

_____ .

Consent:

I, _____, have read and understand the contents of this release form.
(please print name)

I give permission to the school counselor named above, to release school counseling case notes and to freely communicate information shared by the student named above with the professional listed in this document.

Parent/Guardian Signature:_____ Date:_____

Figure 6.12. Releases of school counseling case notes and sharing of information form

SCORE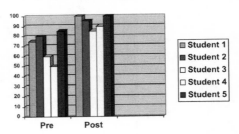

<u>School Counseling Operational Report of Effectiveness</u>

Number/Description of Participants:
Describe Impact and Implications:
Follow-up Plan:

Pre- and Post-Program Measures

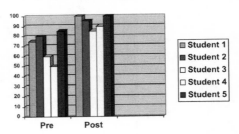

- Student 1
- Student 2
- Student 3
- Student 4
- Student 5

Pre-Post Data
Worksheet

Figure 6.13.   Results report template: School Counseling Operational Report of Effectiveness (SCORE)

Pre- and Post-Program Data Worksheet

Program Title:

Data Type:

Pre-Program Data	Post-Program Data	Pre-Program Data Mean	Post-Program Data Mean	Percentage of Change Pre- to Post-Program
		50	100	100%
50	100			

Figure 6.14.   Pre- and postprogram data worksheet

SCORE allows the user to enhance results reporting with graphic representations. Remember—a picture is worth a thousand words! To complete the graph, double-click on it and modify the content to reflect the data. Like the worksheet, the graph can be deleted, saved in a separate folder on your computer, or be duplicated for multiple graphic representations.

Suicide Ideation Report

School counselors who suspect a child or adolescent may be suicidal should document these cases and make appropriate contacts. The Suicide Ideation Form on the ancillary website (see figure 6.15) walks school counselors through the legally sound reporting processes. If you are required to use your school's form, please look for the following processes in the school's policy or on the form: (1) If a parent can be implicated as a reason for suicide ideation, then the parent should not contacted. Instead, contact Child Protective Services or other agencies identified in your school's policy and share information related to the student implicating the parent, and (2) outside counseling from a professional counselor pertaining to the student's emotional state should be obtained prior to his returning to school. If neither process is a part of your school's policy or forms, please bring this to the attention of your school counseling division director or principal.

SUMMARY

Accountability in education and school counseling practices is a growing trend. Accountable practices necessitate that school counselors create action plans and results reports that identify data-driven, standards-based, and research-supported services, as well as specify program goals, procedures, and evaluative outcomes. Accountability is also established through the daily use of reporting forms, letters, and other communications to demonstrate credible practices and processes that are culturally sensitive and ethically and legally sound.

School Name HERE

Suicide Prevention: Assessment and Reporting
(SCHOOL COUNSELING STUDENTS KNOW YOUR SCHOOL POLICIES AND KNOW THE LAWS IN YOUR STATE)
Students who express thoughts of suicide are considered to be at imminent risk of harm to self or others.

Student Name: _____   Grade: _____
Date of Incident: _____ Time of Incident: _____ Date of Report: _____ Time of Report: _____
School Counselor Reporting: _____
Parent-Guardian: _____ Home Phone: _____ Work/Cell: _____
Student expressed suicidal thoughts: ☐ verbally ☐ in writing ☐ in art ☐ Other
Describe: _____

Current Emotional State

☐ Guilt   ☐ Anxiety   ☐ Sadness   ☐ Flat Affect ☐ Helplessness☐ Other:_____

Describe: _____

Suicide Plan: ☐ Yes or ☐ No   Method: _____   Place: _____   Time: _____
Prior thoughts/threats of suicide? ☐ Yes or ☐ No
Describe: _____
Prior attempt? ☐ Yes or ☐ No   When? _____   Method: _____

Reporting Procedures:

1. Are student's thoughts of suicide related to alleged parental abuse or neglect, or are the parents implicated as a reason for suicide ideation? Yes or No *(if no skip # 2, if yes)*

2. When the parent/legal guardian is implicated as a reason for the student's thought of suicide, **DO NOT** contact the Parent. Contact the Child Protective Services in your city/county at (telephone number HERE).

     Social Services Contact Name: _____   Date: _____ Time: _____
     Describe: _____

3. Parent is contacted and asked if he or she is aware of the student's mental state: Yes   or   No

4. Ask the parent/legal guardian if he or she agrees to obtain professional counseling services for their child. Parents may wish to seek spiritual/religious counseling (see school division policy).

5. If the parent/legal guardian does not agree to obtain professional counseling services, a report is to be made to Child Protective Services, (telephone number HERE).

     Social Services Contact Name: _____   Date: _____ Time: _____
     Describe: _____

6. Keep student supervised until parent/legal guardian or a representative of Child Protective Services arrives. If a parent/legal guardian picks up the student, supply a list of counseling resources and obtain signature on this form.

I am aware that my child has expressed suicidal thoughts and I agree to obtain professional counseling services for my child to include a suicide assessment and safety plan.

_____   _____
Parent or Legal Guardian Signature   Date

Figure 6.15.   Suicide ideation report

Glossary

Adapted from *The School Counselor's Study Guide for Credentialing Exams*, Schellenberg, 2018.

academic development: One of three developmental domains within a comprehensive school counseling program that focuses on promoting skills, relating learning to life, and enhancing academic success and a positive attitude toward school and learning.

access data: Data that assesses inequities in opportunities to participation in rigorous curriculum and school and community programs.

accommodation: Adjustments made to instruction, homework, testing, and the physical environment in order to promote the success of students with special needs (e.g., special education, 504, and ESL students), as well as students with temporary conditions (e.g., illness, injury).

accountability: Practices that are data-driven, standards-based, research-supported, evaluated for effectiveness and ongoing program improvement, and demonstrate "how" school counselors make a difference in the lives of students.

achievement data: In accordance with the ASCA National Model (2012), achievement data is data that assesses students' academic growth.

achievement gap: The disparity in educational performance that exists between specific populations of students—primarily low-income and minority students—when compared to peers on a variety of educational measures, namely standardized tests.

action plan: Written plans that describes specific programming and how programming will achieve stated objectives, including closing the achievement gap activities. SCOPE, the School Counseling Operational Plan for Effectiveness, is an example of ASCA-recommended action plans.

action research: Research conducted for the purpose of enhancing the effectiveness of one's practices and/or measuring program outcomes.

active listening: A basic counseling skill and communication skill that attends to the student's verbal and nonverbal behaviors.

addiction: Psychological and/or physiological dependence on a substance or activity.

advisory council: A committee of stakeholders established by the school counselor to direct and assist the school counseling program. ASCA recommends an advisory committee as part of the school counseling program management system to promote program success.

advocacy: A function of the school counselor that involves acting and speaking on behalf of others to support equity and access to programming and promoting student, family, school, and community relations and development.

aggression: Verbal, physical, and psychological behaviors intended to cause harm, threat, or pain.

Americans with Disabilities Act (ADA): National legislation that prohibits discrimination against persons with a disability in employment, public institutions, public transportation, and telecommunications. A qualified individual with a disability is entitled to reasonable accommodations.

anorexia: An eating disorder that is characterized primarily by a consistent and extreme restriction of food intake and a refusal to maintain a minimum normal body weight for age and height.

antisocial behavior: Behavior, covert and overt, that disregards the rights and privacy of others and the norms, laws, and standards of a society.

appraisal (see also assessment): Approaches and/or measures (standardized and nonstandardized) used to gain a greater understanding of a student's functioning (e.g., intellectual, educational, mental, emotional, social, physical, and occupational).

ASCA National Model: The only national model for the profession of school counseling designed to serve as a framework from which to implement a comprehensive, developmental, and primarily preventative school counseling program.

ASCA National Standards: National standards (a foundational component of the ASCA National Model) that depict what students should know and be able to do as a result of a comprehensive school counseling program in three broad developmental areas: career, academic, and personal/social.

assessment (see also appraisal): Approaches and/or measures (standardized and nonstandardized) used to gain a greater understanding of a student's functioning (e.g., intellectual, educational, mental, emotional, social, physical, and occupational).

attainment data: Data that assesses levels of completion (e.g., graduation rates, attendance rates, college acceptance rates, and course completion rates).

behavior contract: A plan of action used for general education students to reduce or eliminate specific, observable, and measurable undesirable behaviors by applying specific interventions and rewards.

Behavior Intervention Plan (BIP): A plan of action, often part of an IEP for special education students, aimed at reducing or eliminating specific, observable, and measurable undesirable behaviors by applying individualized interventions and rewards.

behavioral data: In accordance with the ASCA National Model (2012), behavioral data is data that literature has found to be linked to academic achievement.

behavioral rehearsal: Practicing new skills and behaviors for application outside of the counseling environment.

bibliotherapy: The use of books/literature in counseling toward established counseling goals.

bulimia: An eating disorder that is characterized primarily by reoccurring episodes of binging and purging (e.g., vomiting, laxatives) and a preoccupation with body weight.

bullying (see also cyberbullying): Any verbal, nonverbal, or physical behavior intended to intimidate, threaten, harm, or cause physical, emotional, and/or psychological pain.

career awareness: The focus on career development at the elementary level that promotes students' knowledge of the world of work.

career counseling: Counseling aimed at career development at a specific time and across the life span.

career development: One of three developmental domains of a comprehensive school counseling program that promotes students' identification of, and preparation for, desired post–high school occupations, education, and training, and relating school to the world of work.

career development inventories: Instruments used to enhance a student's knowledge pertaining to occupational choices, self-knowledge (e.g., interests, values, and skills), and education and training related to specific careers.

career exploration: The focus at the middle school level that enhances students' understanding of career opportunities and the link between school and work and developing an academic plan to meet postsecondary career choices.

career planning: The focus at the high school level that encourages students to continue to update and follow through on established career and academic plans for career readiness.

child abuse: Harm toward a child caused by neglect or exploitation and/or physical, emotional, psychological, or sexual mistreatment.

child neglect: Failure to provide for the social, psychological, emotional, and biological needs of a child; failure to prevent suffering or to act on behalf of the child that places the child in imminent danger; behaviors that place the child in harm's way.

child study: A team approach to identifying and understanding the needs of a student who is not achieving academically in comparison to peers or demonstrating physical, emotional, verbal, or psychological issues that are interfering with daily functioning.

closed group: Groups that are no longer open to new membership once group facilitation begins.

collaboration: A function of the school counselor that involves working cooperatively with others toward a common goal.

Computer-Assisted Career Guidance Systems (CACGS): Electronic systems designed to promote career readiness.

conflict resolution: The process by which students resolve conflict peacefully by engaging a variety of skills (e.g., problem solving, empathy, clarification, questioning, communication, and negotiation).

consultation: A function of school counselors that involves providing services in their area of expertise to other stakeholders (e.g., teachers, parents, and school administrators).

convergent problem solving: Higher order analytical thinking that draws information from resources for a single best solution.

core school counseling curriculum: Planned and documented (e.g., action/lesson plans) curriculum that is comprehensive, developmental, preventative, and delivered to all students as a direct service via instruction and group activities.

crisis: Traumatic or extremely stressful situations that require immediate action to secure the safety and well-being of students and others (e.g., suicide or homicide risk, post-student suicide, homicide, accidental death, terrorism, natural disaster, and child abuse/neglect).

crosswalking: A strategy (and ASCA school counselor competency) that integrates ASCA student standards with other relevant standards such as core academic standards.

cyberbullying (see also bullying): Any electronic (e.g., texting, internet, email, chat rooms, and social networks) behavior intended to intimidate, threaten, harm, or cause physical, emotional, and/or psychological pain.

data analysis: An examination of information that aids school counselors in identifying stakeholder needs, targeting programming, and determining program effectiveness and areas for improvement.

data-driven: Programs, practices, and activities that are created based on an analysis of data.

diagnostic test: An assessment used to identify areas of academic competencies and areas of deficit.

direct student services: Equitable, comprehensive, needs-driven school counseling services that support the personal/social, academic, and career development of all students via the school counseling core curriculum, individual student planning, and responsive services.

disability: A cognitive/psychological, behavioral, and/or physical impairment that limits one or more daily living functions.

disaggregated data: The separation and analysis of data by specific variables to identify student populations who are performing at lower levels and ensure equity and access.

divergent problem solving: Higher order holistic thinking that draws information from fresh, more creative perspectives and across disciplines for multiple possible solutions.

educational diagnostician: An individual employed by school divisions to assess levels of student academic functioning and to suggest interventions to meet individual student needs; often a member of child study teams.

emancipated minor: A minor who has been granted by the courts the decision-making power of an adult with regard to his or her own affairs. Emancipated minors do not need parental consent to engage in counseling services.

encapsulation: Ignorance of one's cultural background and how culture impacts one's total being.

English as a Second Language (ESL): A descriptive term for those whose primary or native language is not English.

equity: Eliminating barriers to rigorous curriculum and school and community programs and promoting systemic policies, practices, and programs that establish and nurture culturally sensitive and culturally responsive environments.

extrinsic motivation: Motivation that is achieved with external rewards (e.g., stickers, certification, treats, or praise).

Family Educational Rights and Privacy Act (FERPA): Legislation enacted to protect the privacy of students' academic records and to allow parents and students to inspect academic records and petition for the removal of information perceived as inaccurate. FERPA is also known as the Buckley Amendment.

504 Plan: A written document that identifies special accommodations afforded to students with qualifying conditions pursuant to Section 504 of the Rehabilitation Act of 1973.

Free and Appropriate Public Education (FAPE): Legislation that ensures individualized curriculum that meets unique student needs and prepares students for post–high school education, careers, and independent living.

General Equivalency Diploma (GED): An alternative to a high school diploma and completion of high school, the GED established mastery of high school core course content and may be obtained during the high school years through alternative educational programs or after high school for those adults who "dropped out" of high school.

Guidance counselor: An outdated title for the counselor in the preK–12 school setting depicting only one component of the many functions of the contemporary school counselor that is associated primarily with more directive approaches and education and career planning.

high-stakes testing: Standardized testing used to determine passing or failing of select core courses for graduation from high school; also drives the type of diploma received.

in loco parentis: A common-law doctrine that allows educators to act as parents, protecting students and their rights while under their care at school.

inclusion classroom: A general education classroom that provides additional supports and accommodations for special education student participation.

indirect student services: Equitable, comprehensive school counseling services that support the personal/social, academic, and career development of all students using referrals for additional assistance/resources; collaboration with parents, educators, and community agencies; and in consultation with others the sharing and receiving of information useful in promoting student academic achievement, development, and well-being.

individual-focused: School counseling practices that are more focused on intervention for a select individual versus prevention and intervention services for all students.

individual student planning: A systemic direct student service that aids students in developing academic, personal, and career strategies for future plans and goal attainment via appraisal and advisement.

Individualized Education Program (IEP): A written document that identifies specific and individualized strategies for the personal/social, academic, and career success of students with a qualifying disability under IDEA as part of special education services.

Individuals with Disabilities Education Act (IDEA): National legislation that ensures that the educational needs of students with disabilities are met.

intelligence quotient (IQ): A score from standardized intelligence tests that represents one's level of intelligence.

intelligence test: Standardized tests intended to assess an individual's cognitive abilities and yield an intelligence quotient score.

intervention: Activities and strategies applied with the purpose of reducing or eliminating specific thoughts, actions, or situations.

intrinsic motivation: Motivation that is achieved with internal rewards (e.g., specific positive feedback, earned recognition through accomplishment).

leadership: The ability to inspire, influence, and persuade others to follow or act.

learning profile: A comprehensive conceptualization that considers an individual's learning styles, predisposition toward specific intelligences (see multiple intelligences), and cultural and gender differences.

least restrictive environment: Special education students are to receive educational services that promote success in the least restrictive manner while receiving accommodations and supports as outlined in the student's IEP; least restrictive environments in the public-school setting are the general education classrooms (see also inclusion classroom).

Limited English Proficient (LEP): Individuals whose first language is not English and are therefore restricted in their English-speaking ability.

medical plan: Used in schools for students with medical conditions that might warrant special accommodations for a specified amount of time.

Mindsets and Behaviors for Student Success: Thirty-five standards based on research and best practices and published by ASCA that identify knowledge, skills, and attitudes to achieve student success in three broad categories of academic, career, and social/emotional development.

modeling: Observing and imitating others.

motivation: A force, energy, desire, or state of being that directs thoughts and behavior.

multicultural counseling: Counseling that is sensitive to the needs of all people and their unique worldviews grounded in gender, race, ethnicity, culture, social status, economic status, sexual orientation, and religion.

multiple intelligences: Eight independent cognitive and affective intelligences working interactively for a holistic understanding of human intelligence.

needs assessment: Formal information measures that result in the identification of stakeholder needs.

negative reinforcement: Removal of a stimulus in an effort to increase a desired behavior/response.

New Vision School Counseling: The movement to transform school counseling into an academic- and systems-focused paradigm.

No Child Left Behind (NCLB): Legislation that supports standards-based education, the measurement of goals to enhance academic outcomes, and closing achievement gaps between specific classes and racial groups of students.

nontraditional occupation: Occupations in which few individuals of a specific gender generally work. For example, occupations historically dominated by females would be nontraditional occupations for males (e.g., nurse), and occupations historically dominated by males would be nontraditional for females (e.g., mechanic).

Occupational Information Network (O*Net): National database for career information, exploration, assessment, and career decision making.

Occupational Outlook Handbook (OOH): Nationally recognized source for career information and career decision making.

open group: Groups that allow new membership once group facilitation begins.

outcome evaluation/data: Program evaluation/data that assesses the effectiveness of a program/activity in meeting established goals and objectives.

paraphrasing: A basic counseling technique that involves the school counselor restating what a student has shared to communicate understanding.

peer helping: Programs that involve students helping students (e.g., peer tutoring, peer mentoring, and peer mediation).

peer mediation: A process by which students help students to resolve conflict peacefully by engaging a variety of skills (e.g., problem solving, empathy, clarification, questioning, communication, and negotiation). Peer mediation involves more than two individuals.

perception evaluation/data: Program evaluation/data that assesses participants' opinions about their own thoughts, beliefs, feelings, and abilities.

personal–social development: One of three developmental domains within a comprehensive school counseling program that promotes total student well-being through the application of counseling theory and techniques and teaches skills for living (e.g., safety, problem solving, decision making, conflict resolution, and communication).

play therapy: The use of directive and nondirective play facilitated by the school counselor as a therapeutic medium for emotional expression and communication.

positive reinforcement: Application of a stimulus to increase a desired behavior/response.

prevention: Activities and strategies applied with the purpose of averting specific thoughts, actions, or situations.

primary prevention: Programming that focuses on prevention and wellness for a large population (e.g., entire student body) who may or may not be potentially at risk for a specific targeted behavior/problem.

process evaluation/data: Program evaluation/data that describes the event/program and the number of participants impacted by the activity.

professional associations: School counseling–related associations that support the profession with resources, professional development opportunities, unification, and advocacy.

professional school counselor: The former title for the school counselor in the preK–12 school setting that followed the title of guidance counselor.

program evaluation: An ongoing component of accountable school counseling practices that results in data that demonstrate program outcomes and answers the question "How do school counselors make a difference in the lives of students?" and provides information for program improvement.

reciprocal determinism: A term coined by Albert Bandura to describe how behavior is determined by the shared relationship (one acting upon the other) between a person and the environment.

reinforcement/reinforcer (see also negative reinforcement; positive reinforcement): A concept used in operant conditioning to refer to a stimulus, positive or negative, that increases the likelihood of desired behaviors or reduces/eliminates undesired behaviors.

research-based: School counseling practices and programming that are supported by research.

resilience: The capacity of an individual to cope with stress and harsh conditions.

response to intervention: An intervention process used to help struggling students to improve behavior and achieve academically.

responsive services: Direct student services that meet the immediate needs and concerns of students, including crisis response via short-term, goal-focused individual and small-group counseling.

results report: Written reports that describe the outcomes of specific programming as outlined in action plans, including closing the achievement gap activities. SCORE, the School Counseling Operational Report of Effectiveness, is an example of an ASCA-recommended results report.

risk factors: Any physical, personal, social, familial, environmental, or economic condition that places students at a disadvantage and serves as an obstacle to well-being, academic achievement, and healthy student development.

school counselor: The contemporary title of the counselor in the school who embraces and implements a comprehensive counseling program that shares the dual roles of educator and counselor and practices using a comprehensive developmental model with an academic and systems-focused mindset.

school nurse: An individual employed by school divisions to attend to student injury; coordinate medical care with physicians, psychologists, and parents; and administer medications during the school day; often a member of child study teams.

school psychologist: An individual employed by school divisions to assess levels of student psychological functioning and suggest interventions to meet individual student needs; often a member of child study teams.

school social worker: An individual employed by school divisions to assess levels of student social and family functioning and suggest interventions to meet individual student needs; often a member of child study teams.

School-to-Work Opportunities Act: Legislation that seeks to ensure that students will be well prepared to succeed in our multifaceted and technologically advanced workforce.

secondary prevention: Programming aimed at mediating a specific behavior or problem that has been identified as a potential threat among a particular population or subgroup of students.

social justice: A moral and ethical movement toward creating a socially just world through an equitable distribution of resources to ensure personal, social, career, and academic development and well-being.

social responsibility: A moral and ethical ideology that is grounded in the principles of equality, unity, respect for human rights, and acting on behalf of the good of a society.

Socratic dialogue: Inquiry or questioning aimed at exploring an individual's thoughts and/or knowledge pertaining to a specific topic.

special needs students: Students who are limited English proficient or have a 504 plan or IEP.

standards: Statements that delineate what students should know and be able to do.

strengths-based counseling: A counseling approach that emphasizes the value of protective factors in combating risk factors and enhancing resilience.

Section 504: A part of the Americans with Disabilities Act (ADA), also known as the Rehabilitation Act of 1973, that protects individuals with disabilities from discrimination and allows for equal access to services and the provision of reasonable accommodations related to the disability.

stakeholders: Any individual/organization that impacts or is impacted by the school.

Student Council Association: A program sponsored by educators to develop students' leadership and interpersonal skills while promoting school and community spirit and involvement.

substance abuse: Repeated use of a chemical substance that may or may not include dependence.

substance use: Repeated use of a chemical substance without dependence.

suicide assessment: Screening individuals to determine their risk for suicide.

suicide ideation: Thinking about taking one's own life.

summarizing: A basic counseling technique whereby the school counselor condenses into a few brief statements that which the student has conveyed over a period of time during the counseling session.

systems-focused: School counseling practices that are more focused on prevention and intervention services for all students versus a select few.

teaming: Joining together with other stakeholders to accomplish a common goal.

tertiary prevention: Programming that targets a specific population that is already engaging in at-risk behavior or experiencing a specific problem in order to reduce or eliminate the problem or behavior and improve quality of life.

Transforming School Counseling Initiative (TSCI): The movement to change the paradigm of school counseling to one that is academic- and systems-focused.

universal academic achievement: Academic achievement for all students.

wellness: A sense of personal, social, emotional, physical, and spiritual well-being.

worldview: How individuals conceptualize and interpret the world, view their relationship with the world, and interact with a world that is grounded in presupposition, beliefs, and values.

zeitgeist: The thought or spirit of the time in a specified time period or generation.

References

Agnew, T., Vaught, C., Getz, H., & Fortune, J. (2000). Peer group clinical supervision program fosters confidence and professionalism. *Professional School Counseling, 4,* 6–12.

American Counseling Association (ACA). (1987). *School counseling: A profession at risk.* Alexandria, VA: Author.

American Counseling Association (ACA). (2005). *Code of ethics and standards of practice.* Alexandria, VA: Author.

American Evaluation Association. (1994). Guiding principles for evaluators. *New Directions for Program Evaluation, 66,* 19–26.

American School Counselor Association. (2017). *ASCA position statement.* Retrieved January 21, 2019, from www.schoolcounselor.org.

American School Counselor Association (ASCA). (2016a). *Ethical standards for school counselors.* Alexandria, VA: Author.

American School Counselor Association (ASCA). (2016b). *The ASCA national model implementation guide.* Alexandria, VA: Author.

American School Counselor Association (ASCA). (2014). *Mindsets and behaviors for student success: K-12 college- and career-readiness standards for every student.* Alexandria, VA: Author.

American School Counselor Association. (2012). *ASCA national model: A framework for school counseling programs* (3rd ed.). Alexandria, VA: Author.

Anderson, L. W., & Krathwohl, D. R. (Eds.). (2001). *A taxonomy for learning, teaching, and assessing: A revision of Bloom's Taxonomy of educational objectives.* New York, NY: Longman.

Anni, C. T., Sunawan, & Haryono. (2018). School counselor's intention to use technology: The technology acceptance model. *The Turkish Online Journal of Educational Technology, 17*(2), 120–124.

Arbuckle, D. S. (1961). The conflicting functions of the school counselor. *Counselor Education and Supervision, 1,* 54–59.

Association for Assessment in Counseling and Education. (1998). *Competencies in assessment and evaluation for school counselors.* Retrieved from http://aace.ncat.edu.

Auger, R. W. (2004). Responding to terror: The impact of September 11 on K–12 schools and schools' responses. *Professional School Counseling, 7,* 222–231.

Bardhoshi, G., Duncan, K., & Erford, B. T. (2017). Effect of a specialized classroom counseling intervention on increasing self-efficacy among first-grade rural students. *Professional School Counseling, 21*(1), 12–25.

Beale, A. V. (1995). Selecting school counselors: The principal's perspective. *The School Counselor, 42*, 211–217.

Bloom, B. S. (1953). Thought processes in lectures and discussions. *Journal of General Education, 7*, 160–169.

Bohecker, L, Schellenberg, R., & Silvey, R. (2017). Spirituality and religion: The ninth CACREP common core curricular area. *Counseling & Values, 62*(2), 128–143.

Bowers, H., Lemberger-Truelove, M. E., & Brigman, G. (2017). A social-emotional leadership framework for school counselors. *Professional School Counseling, 21*(1b), 21–31.

Briggs, M. K., Akos, P., Czyszczon, G., & Eldridge, A. (2011). Assessing and promoting spiritual wellness as a protective factor in secondary schools. *Counseling and Values, 55* (2), 171–184.

Brigman, G., Villares, E., & Webb, L. (2017). *Evidence-based school counseling: A student success approach.* Taylor & Francis/Routledge Publishing.

Brougham, L., & Kashubeck-West, S. (2017). Impact of growth mindset intervention on academic performance of students in two urban high schools. *Professional School Counseling, 21*(1), 1–9.

Brown, C. H., Olivarez, A., & Dekruyf, L. (2018). The impact of the school counselor supervision model on the self-efficacy of school counselor site supervisors. *Professional School Counseling, 21*(1), 152–160.

Bryan, J. (2005). Fostering educational resilience and achievement in urban schools through school-family-community partnerships. *Professional School Counseling, 8*, 219–228.

Burnham, J. J., & Jackson, C. M. (2000). School counselor roles: Discrepancies between actual practice and existing models. *Professional School Counseling, 4*, 41–49.

Cahill, M. J., McDaniel, M. A., Frey, R. F., Hynes, K. M., Repice, M., Zhao, J., & Trousil, R. (2018). Understanding the relationship between student attitudes and student learning. *Physical Review Physics Education Research, 14*(1), 1–10.

Campbell, C. A., & Dahir, C. A. (1997). *Sharing the vision: The national standards for school counseling programs.* Alexandria, VA: American School Counselor Association Press.

Center for School Counseling Outcome Research and Evaluation. (2000). Retrieved from www.umass.edu/schoolcounseling.

Cholewa, B., Goodman-Scott, E., Thomas, A., & Cook, J. (2016). Teachers' perceptions and experiences consulting with school counselors: A qualitative study. *Professional School Counseling, 21*(1), 77–88.

Cooper, B. S. (2002). *Promises and perils facing today's superintendents.* New York, NY: Rowman & Littlefield.

Council for Accreditation of Counseling and Related Educational Programs (CACREP). (2016). *CACREP accreditation standards and procedures manual* (5th ed.). Alexandria, VA: Author.

Crutchfield, L. B., & Borders, L. D. (1997). Impact of two clinical peer supervision models on practicing school counselors. *Journal of Counseling and Development, 75*, 219–230.

Dilley, J., Foster, W., & Bowers, I. (1973). Effectiveness ratings of counselors without teaching experience. *Counselor Education and Supervision, 13*, 24–29.

Dobmeier, R. A. (2011). School counselors support student spirituality through developmental assets, character education, and ASCA competency indicators. *Professional School Counseling, 14*, 317–327.

Dong, J., Hwang, W., Shadiev, R., & Chen, G. (2017). Pausing the classroom lecture: The use of clickers to facilitate student engagement. *Active Learning in Higher Education, 18*(2), 157–172.

Duarte, D., & Hatch, T. (2015). Successful implementation of a federally funded violence prevention elementary school counseling program: Results bring sustainability. *Professional School Counseling, 18*(1), 71–81.

The Education Trust. (1997). *The national guidance and counseling reform program.* Washington, DC: Author.

Eschenauer, R., & Hayes, C. (2005). The transformative individual school counseling model: An accountability model for urban school counselors. *Professional School Counseling, 8,* 244–249.

Farmer, L. B. (2017). An examination of counselors' religiosity, spirituality, and lesbian-, gay-, bisexual-affirmation counselor competence. *Professional Counselor, 7*(2), 114–128.

Flett, G. L., & Hewitt, P. L. (2013). Disguised distress in children and adolescents "flying under the radar": Why psychological problems are underestimated and how schools must respond. *Canadian Journal of School Psychology, 28*(1), 12–27.

Gallo, L. L. (2014). Spirituality and school counselor education and supervision. *Journal of School Counseling, 12*(6), 3–21.

Gallo, L. L., Rausch, M., Smith, C. K., & Wood, S. (2015). School counselors' experiences working with digital natives: A qualitative study. *Professional School Counseling, 20*(1), 14–24.

Gardner, H. (1983). *Frames of mind: The theory of multiple intelligences.* New York, NY: Basic Books.

Gardner, H., & Moran, S. (2006). The science of multiple intelligences theory: A response to Lynn Waterhouse. *Educational Psychologist, 41*(4), 227–232.

Gladding, S. T. (2001). *The counseling dictionary.* Upper Saddle River, NJ: Merrill-Prentice Hall.

Goddard, R. D., Hoy, W. K., & Woolfolk, H. A. (2000). Collective teacher efficacy: Its meaning, measure, and impact on student achievement. *American Educational Research Journal, 37,* 479–507.

Goodman-Scott, E., Betters-Bubon, J., & Donohue, P. (2016). Aligning comprehensive school counseling programs and positive behavioral interventions and supports to maximize school counselors' efforts. *Professional School Counseling, 19*(1), 57–67.

Goodrich, A. (2018). Peer mentoring and peer tutoring among K–12 students: A literature review. *Applications of Research in Music Education, 36*(2), 13–21.

Guerra, P. (1998). Reaction to DeWitt Wallace grant overwhelming: Readers sound off on February *Counseling Today* article. *Counseling Today,* April, 13–20.

Hardesty, P. H., & Dillard, J. M. (1994). Analysis of activities of school counselors. *Psychological Reports, 74,* 447–450.

Havlik, S. A., Rowley, P., Puckett, J., Wilson, G., & Neasen, E. (2017). Do whatever you can to try to support that kid. *Professional School Counseling, 21*(1), 47–59.

Houser, R. (1998). *Counseling and educational research.* Thousand Oaks, CA: Sage.

Kaffenberger, C. J., Murphy, S., & Bemak, F. (2006). School counseling leadership team: A statewide collaborative model to transform school counseling. *Professional School Counseling, 9,* 288–295.

Kamrath, B., & Brooker, T. (2017). Improved attitude and achievement: A case study of an elementary school academic advisement intervention. *Professional School Counseling, 21*(1), 60–69.

Kennedy, S. D., & Stanley, B. B. (2015). School counseling websites: Do they have content that serves diverse students? *Professional School Counseling, 18*(1), 49–60.

Kerby, A. T., & Wroughton, J. R. (2017). When do students' attitudes change? Investigating student attitudes at midterm. *Statistics Education Research Journal, 16*(2), 476–486.

Kim, J., Fletcher, K., & Bryan, J. (2018). Empowering marginalized parents: An emerging parent empowerment model for school counselors. *Professional School Counseling, 21*(1b), 1–9.

Kimbel, T., & Schellenberg, R. (2014). Meeting the holistic needs of students: A proposal for spiritual and religious competencies for school counselors. *Professional School Counseling, 17*(1), 76–85.

Kitchener, K. S. (1984). Intuition, critical evaluation, and ethical principles: The foundation for ethical decisions in counseling psychology. *Counseling Psychologist, 12*(3), 43–55.

Kneal, M. G., Young, A., & Dollarhide, C. T. (2017). Cultivating school counseling leaders through district leadership cohorts. *Professional School Counseling, 21*(1b), 12–18.

Magaldi-Dopman, D., & Park-Taylor, J. (2014). Integration amidst separation: Religion, urban education, and the first amendment. *Urban review: Issues and ideas in public education, 46*(1), 47–62.

Marzano, R. J. (2004). *Building background knowledge for academic achievement: Research on what works in schools.* Alexandria, VA: Association for Supervision and Curriculum Development.

Mason, E. C., Land, C., Brodie, I., Collins, K., Pennington, C., Sands, K., & Sierra, M. (2016). Data and research that matter: Mentoring school counselors to publish action research. *Professional School Counseling, 20*(1), 184–193.

Matteson. S. M. (2014). Ghost children: Invisible middle level students. *Middle Grades Research Journal, 9*(2), 19–35.

Mayes, R. D., Dollarhide, C. T., & Young, A. (2018). School counselors as leaders in school turnaround. *Journal of Organizational and Educational Leadership, 4*(1), 1–23.

McLeod, D. A., Jones, R., & Cramer, E. P. (2015). An evaluation of a school-based, peer-facilitated, healthy relationship program for at-risk adolescents. *Children & Schools, 37*(2), 108–116.

Merlin, C., & Brendel, J. M. (2017). A supervision training program for school counseling site supervisors. *The Clinical Supervisor, 36*(2), 304–323.

Michel, R. E., Lorelle, S., & Atkins, K. M. (2017). LEAD with data: A model for school counselors in training. *Professional School Counseling, 21*(1b), 32–38.

Milsom, A., & McCormick, K. (2016). Evaluating an accountability mentoring approach for school counselors. *Professional School Counseling, 19*(1), 27–35.

Moles, O. C. (1993). Collaboration between schools and disadvantaged parents: Obstacles and openings. In N. Chavkin (Ed.), *Families and schools in a pluralistic society.* Albany, NY: State University of New York Press.

Moran, K., & Bodenhorn, M. (2015). Elementary school counselors' collaboration with community mental health providers. *Journal of School Counseling, 13*(4), 1–33.

Myrick, R. D. (2003). Accountability: Counselors count. *Professional School Counseling, 6,* 174–189.

National Council of Teachers of English (NCTE). (1996). *Standards for the English language arts.* Newark, DE: International Reading Association.

National Council of Teachers of Mathematics (NCTM). (2000). Principles and standards for school mathematics. Reston, VA: Author.

No Child Left Behind Act of 2001, Pub. L. No. 107–110.

Olson, M. J., & Allen, D. N. (1993). Principals' perceptions of the effectiveness of school counselors with and without teaching experience. *Counselor Education and Supervision, 33,* 10–21.

Page, B. J., Pietrzak, D. R., & Sutton, J. M. (2001). National survey of school counselor supervision. *Counselor Education and Supervision, 41,* 142–151.

Paisley, P. O., & Hayes, R. L. (2003). School counseling in the academic domain: Transformations in preparation and practice. *Professional School Counseling, 6,* 198–205.

Peterson, J. S., Goodman, R., Keller, T., & McCauley, A. (2004). Teachers and non-teachers as school counselors: Reflections on the internship experience. *Professional School Counseling, 7,* 246–256.

Pierce, G. L., & Cleary, P. F. (2016). The K-12 educational technology value chain: Aps for kidds, tools for teachers, and levers for reform. *Education and Information Technologies, 21*(4), 863–880.

Posavac, E. J., & Carey, R. G. (2003). *Program evaluation: Methods and case studies* (6th ed.). Upper Saddle River, NJ: Prentice Hall.

Poynton, T. A., & Carey, J. C. (2006). An integrative model of data-based decision making for school counseling. *Professional School Counseling, 10,* 121–131.

Remley, T., & Herlihy, B. (2014). *Ethical, legal, and professional issues in counseling* (4th ed.). Upper Saddle River, NJ: Pearson.

Ritchie, M., & Bobby, C. (2011). *Working together hand-in-hand: The common goals of CACREP and state counselor licensure boards.* A presentation at NBCC's 2011 State Licensure Board Meeting, Greensboro, NC.

Rosheim, K. C., (2018). A cautionary tale about using the word "shy": An action research study of how three quiet learners demonstrated participation beyond speech. *Journal of Adolescent & Adult Literacy, 51*(5), 663–670.

Schellenberg, R. (2007). Standards blending: Aligning school counseling programs with school academic achievement missions. *Virginia Counselors Journal, 29,* 13–20.

Schellenberg, R. (2018). *The school counselor's desk reference and credentialing examination study guide.* Taylor & Francis/Routledge Publishing.

Schellenberg, R., & Grothaus, T. (2009). Promoting cultural responsiveness and closing the achievement gap with standards blending. *Professional School Counseling, 12,* 440–449.

Schellenberg, R., & Grothaus, T. (2011). Using culturally competent responsive services to improve student achievement and behavior. *Professional School Counseling, 14,* 222–230.

Schellenberg, R., Parks-Savage, A., & Rehfuss, M. (2007). Reducing levels of elementary school violence with peer mediation. *Professional School Counseling, 10,* 475–481.

Search Institute. (2007). Developmental assets list. Retrieved from www.search-institute.org/developmental-assets/lists.

Shields, C. M. (2016). *Transformative Leadership: Primer.* New York, NY: Peter Lang.

Shields, C. M., Dollarhide, C., & Young, A. (2017). Transformative leadership in school counseling: An emerging paradigm for equity and excellence. *Professional School Counseling, 21*(1b), 1–11.

Shimoni, A., & Greenberger, L. (2015). School counselors deliver information about school counseling and their work: What professional message is conveyed? *Professional School Counseling, 18*(1), 15–27.

Shoffner, M. F., & Williamson, R. D. (2000). Engaging preservice school counselors and principals in dialogue and collaboration. *Counselor Education and Supervision, 40,* 128–141.

Sink, C. (2005). *Contemporary school counseling: Theory, research, and practice.* Boston, MA: Houghton Mifflin.

Sink, C. (2011). School-wide responsive services and the value of collaboration. *Professional School Counseling, 14*, ii–iv.

Sink, C. (2018). Program evaluation in doctoral-level counselor education preparation: Concerns and recommendations. *American Journal of Evaluation, 39*(4), 496–510.

Sink, C., & Devlin, J. M. (2011). Student spirituality and school counseling: Issues, opportunities, and challenges. *Counseling and Values, 55*(2), 130–148.

Snow, W. H., Lamar, M. R., Hinkle, J. S., & Speciale, M. (2018). Current practices in online counselor education. *Professional Counselor, 8*(2), 131–145.

Steele, T. M., Jacokes, D. E., & Stone, C. B. (2015). An examination of the role of online technology in school counseling. *Professional School Counseling, 18*(1), 125–135.

Stein, K. C., Miness, A., & Kintz, T. (2018). Teachers' cognitive flexibility on engagement and their ability to engage students: A theoretical and empirical exploration. *Teachers College Records, 120*(6), 1–38.

Stone, C. (2009). *School counseling principles, ethics, and law.* Alexandria, VA: American School Counseling Association.

Sutton, C. M. (2006). The leader's role in reaching universal success for all. *School Administrator, 63*, 47.

Tarbutton, T. (2018). Leveraging 21st-century learning and technology to create caring diverse classroom cultures. *Multicultural Education, 25*(2), 4–6.

U.S. Department of Education. (1996). *Companion document: Crosscutting guidance for the Elementary and Secondary Education Act.* Washington, DC: Author.

U.S. Department of Education. (2004). *Helping practitioners meet the goals of No Child Left Behind.* Washington, DC: Author.

U.S. House of Representatives 109th Congress. (2006). House Report 109–143, Departments of Labor, Health and Human Services, and Education, and Related Agencies. Appropriation Bill, 2006. Washington, DC: Library of Congress.

Van Horn, S. M., & Myrick, R. D. (2001). Computer technology and the 21st century school counselor. *Professional School Counseling, 5*, 124–130.

Vansteenkiste, M., Lens, W., & Deci, E. L. (2006). Intrinsic versus extrinsic goal contents in self-determination theory: Another look at the quality of academic motivation. *Educational Psychologist, 41*, 19–29.

Watkinson, J. S., Goodman-Scott, E. C., Martin, I., & Biles, K. (2018). Counselor educators' experiences preparing preservice school counselors: A phenological study. *Counselor Education and Supervision, 57*(3), 178–193.

White, F. A. (2007). The professional school counselor's challenge: Accountability. *Journal of Professional Counseling, Practice, Theory, and Research, 35*(2), 62–70.

Young, A., Dollarhide, C. T., Baughman, A. (2016). The voices of school counselors: Essential characteristics of school counselor leaders. *Professional School Counseling, 19*(1), 36–45.

Young, A., & Kaffenberger, C. (2016). School counseling professional development: Assessing the use of data to inform school counseling services. *Professional School Counseling, 19*(1), 46–56.

Index

abbreviations, xiii

ACA. *See* American Counseling Association (ACA)

academic achievement: aligning counseling with, 40–44, 67; Bloom's learning levels, 22, 24; closing gaps in, 44–46; Gardner's theory of intelligences, 21–22; of invisible students, x; learning environment preferences, 23; learning styles, 23; Marzano's instructional strategies, 22–23; mental health model *vs.* systems-focused model, 26–27; Mindsets and Behaviors for Student Success, xi, 9, 40–44; well-being correlated with, 31

academic-focused school counseling: barriers to, 10; school administration's alliances with, 2, 11–12; shifting to, 12

accountability, 48, 55, 75, 91. *See also* tools for school counselors

ACES (Association for Counselor Education and Supervision), 6–7

acronyms, xiii

action plans, 75, 76

advocacy, 65–67

American Counseling Association (ACA): Association for Counselor Education and Supervision, 6–7; ethical guidelines, 52; "School Counseling: A Profession at Risk", 2, 3; Standards of Practice, 52

American School Counselor Association (ASCA): ASCA Scene, 10; ASCA U Specialist Trainings program, 10; ethical guidelines, 32–33, 47, 52; functions, 9–10, 25; Mindsets and Behaviors for Student Success, xi, 9, 40–44; Position Statements, 32; *Professional School Counseling*, 32; qualifications of school counselor supervisors, 72; results reporting recommendations, 88; School Counselor Competencies, 32; technology guidance, 65. *See also* ASCA national model

Arbuckle, D. S., 39

ASCA national model: advisory council recommendations, 13; CACREP standards and, 6, 9; evidence of outcomes in, 2; goals and objectives of, 19; importance of, ix, 1, 3, 8. *See also* American School Counselor Association (ASCA); standards blending

Association for Counselor Education and Supervision (ACES), 6–7

behavioral interventions, 27–28, 29

Bloom, Benjamin S., 22, 24, 57

About the Author

Rita Schellenberg is nationally recognized for her outstanding achievements in education and school counseling. She is full professor for the CACREP-accredited school counseling program at Liberty University in Virginia and is a school counseling representative for the Virginia Association for Counselor Education and Supervision (VACES). She received her training in school counseling from the College of William and Mary in Virginia. She was named outstanding graduate in her Ph.D. program in counselor education and supervision, and in 2010 she was named one of the top fifteen school counselors in the nation by the American School Counselor Association (ASCA).

Dr. Schellenberg is a licensed school counselor and a licensed professional counselor (LPC). She also holds the credentials of certified clinical mental health counselor (CCMHC), approved clinical supervisor (ACS), national certified counselor (NCC), and national certified school counselor (NCSC). She is certified by ASCA as a school counseling legal and ethical specialist.

Dr. Schellenberg presents regularly across the country on topics related to counseling and has multiple journal publications in peer-reviewed journals such as *Professional School Counseling* and *Counseling and Values*. She has written multiple books, including *The School Counselor's Desk Reference and Credentialing Examination Study Guide*, which was endorsed by an ASCA past president.

Dr. Schellenberg engages in consulting for schools and performance consulting for agencies seeking to enhance the performance of children and adolescents. If you would like more information about her, please visit www.CultivatingPerformance.com.